Wh… are … about this book…

"This book is chock-full of tips and advice. It's like attending a gazillion "Mom groups" without leaving your house. Every point of view is expressed with so much practical and valuable info. A fun and easy read, it's perfect if you have a busy lifestyle (as most parents do) or a short attention span. There is nothing complicated... just straight-forward info from other people who have "been there." I really enjoyed reading this book and would recommend it to all moms!"

-**Diane Lang**, MA Author of *Baby Steps: the Path from Motherhood to Career* and President of www.DLCounseling.com

"As a doctor and soon-to-be mother, this book not only provides trusted information from true experts (moms), but reassurance that there is hope for me to figure it all out!"

-**Keegan Sheridan**, Licensed Naturopathic Doctor

"Each entry is easy-to-read and tips are well-organized covering all the important topics."

-**Gary & Anne Marie Ezzo**, Authors

"Cozy up on the couch with this book and feel as if you were seated with all the other moms in the world, sharing in the experience of motherhood. Filled with practical advice and wisdom from seasoned moms...this book is a must read for every expectant and new mom!"

-**Erin Chase**, Author of *The $5 Dinner Mom Cookbook* and Founder of www.5DollarDinners.com

The Best Advice for New Moms

THE BEST ADVICE FOR NEW MOMS

Time-Saving Tips And Short Stories From Moms Around The World

Jill Clair

edgehill publishing

Nashville, TN | Ann Arbor, MI

The Best Advice for New Moms: Time-Saving Tips and Short Stories from Moms Around the World
By Jill Clair

Published by: Edgehill Publishing, PO Box 95, Dexter, MI 48130

Author's Note: Throughout this book, I have drawn heavily on advice and examples from other mothers; however, to protect their privacy, some names and details have been purposely altered and disguised.

Visit **www.TheBestAdviceForNewMoms.com** for more information, tips, resources and strategies designed to help you in your new role as a mom.

Warning—Disclaimer

This book is designed to provide information on parenting. It is sold with the understanding that the publisher and author are not engaged in rendering legal, accounting or other professional services. If legal or other expert assistance is required, the services of a competent professional should be sought. It is not the purpose of this book to reprint all of the information that is otherwise available to parents, but instead to complement, amplify and supplement other texts. You are urged to read all the available material, learn as much as possible about being a new mother and parenting and tailor the information to your individual needs. Parenting is not a "one-size-fits-all" experience. Anyone who decides to become a new mom must expect to invest a lot of time and effort in it. Every effort has been made to make this book as complete and accurate as possible. However, there may be mistakes, both typographical and in content. Therefore, this text should be used only as a general guide and not as the ultimate source of information on being a new mother or parent. Furthermore, this book contains information on the experience of new mothers and parenting that is current only up to the printing date. The purpose of this book is to educate and to entertain. The author or publisher shall have neither liability nor responsibility to any person or entity with respect to any loss or damage caused, or alleged to have been caused, directly or indirectly, by the information, writing, examples and opinions contained in this book. If you do not wish to be bound by the above, you may return this book to the publisher for a full refund.

If you find any typographical errors in this book, they are there for a reason. Some people love looking for them and we strive to please as many people as possible.

Cover by Elizabeth Workman. Interior by Stephen Caine, www.acquiredesign.com. Photography by Elaine Lee, www.elaineleephotography.com

ISBN 978-0-615-41033-3
First Edition, 2011
Printed in the United States of America.

10 9 8 7 6 5 4 3 2 1

Dedicated to my mom, Lynn Petersen.

I would not be the mom I am today without your example.
Thank you for your consistent love and dedication.
It is the best gift I could ever receive.

Contents

Acknowledgements

There is absolutely no way I could write this book without the help and support from many friends and family.

First and foremost, I want to give a huge thank-you to my wonderful husband, Nathan. I would not be able to complete this crazy endeavor without your love and encouragement from day one. I love doing life with you and can't imagine it any other way!

To my daughters, Kylan and Hadley, I love being your mom and thank you for the joy you bring to my life every day.

I wish to extend a huge, heartfelt thank you to *all* of the wonderful moms who took the time and contributed their advice and stories used in this book. There are too many to mention by name, but this book is a hundred times greater because of you.

For my own mom, Lynn, and my sisters, Amy and Lisa; I thank you for loving me and my girls. Family is so important to me and I love it when we're all together (even in tight places). Thanks, Mom, for all your feedback in the book. I couldn't have done it without you.

For my Dad, who passed away in 2003, I wish he was still here to meet my girls and to see the book completed. Dad, I miss you more than you know.

I'm so grateful for my mom-in-law, Dorothy, who came to my rescue numerous times to watch the girls for me while I worked on the book and who helped with the editing, too. And for my dad-in-law, Craig, who is always so supportive and giving. Love you guys!

Thank you to Sandy Koepke, one of my favorite relatives, for reading the book. Your laughter through parts of the book encouraged me to keep going with this project.

I thank my wonderful editors, Alison Peterson, who got me off to a great start even while she was caring for her sweet newborn at the same time. And Lisa Taylor, I thank you for all your wise feedback and insights to get me to completion. And finally to Sara Hilton; there are no words to fully say how much I am thankful for your friendship and editing brilliance! BAM!

To my designers, Elizabeth Workman and Stephen Caine. I found gems when I found both of you and I'm so thankful for your creative work.

To Elaine Lee, an amazing photographer. Thank you for the energy and life you bring through your work. I am thrilled to have met you.

To Kendy Konecky, your friendship that began in college has meant the world to me! Thank you for your encouragement and help throughout this entire book process. I'm looking forward to reading your book someday!

A special thanks to Shelle Carrig who helped me in the very early stages and led me in the right direction to a great editor and designer. Go Husker Frogs!

To Lindsey Hoelter and Amy Bowman who took the time to read and give feedback on the book even with a busy life and schedule. You are moms I truly admire.

And to Sara Slimp, who pushes me forward and helps me dream bigger than I ever have before.

And lastly, a very special thank you to John Eggen of Mission Publishing. With John's mentoring and teaching, I learned what I needed to know about writing a book and making it a reality. Thank you!

Introduction

I think the first day I realized that having a kid was going to be harder than I thought was the day after I gave birth.

My doctor came into my hospital room for a routine visit, and I remember saying to him, "We did it!" implying that I'd made it through the *hard* part. "I'm alive!" I exclaimed. "I survived giving birth with very little pain medication!"

I will never forget his response. He chuckled and said, "Oh, that was the *easy* part. You have only just begun."

He was right. Nothing had sufficiently prepared me for my new role as a mother. I had lots of head knowledge but soon realized that babies don't arrive "one-size-fits-all." Rather, all newborns are unique and have varying individual needs. No matter how much I thought I knew, I quickly realized that one single plan wasn't going to fit every child. So I've learned to give myself a bit of grace as I discover how to best meet the needs of my little one.

Because all moms' experiences are different, this book offers various, and sometimes conflicting, advice from moms all over the world.

As special as each and every newborn is, so too are their moms. The mothers who contributed advice to this book include brand-new moms, single moms, soccer moms, moms of multiples, CEO moms, yoga moms, PTA moms, and more.

In the pages that follow you will find time-saving tips, fresh ideas, and laugh-out-loud stories. I hope the tricks and tips we share will help you create an ideal balance of form, function, and freewheeling fun. The practical advice in these pages will give you improved self-confidence in your new role, a fool-proof methodology for solving unruly behaviors, an enlightened attitude, and a brand new BMW in a style and color of your choosing. Well, maybe not. But hopefully you will find inspiration, camaraderie, and ideas to help you along in your journey.

Although it's always good to hear what has and hasn't worked for other moms, at some point *you* will have to figure out what's best for you and your baby. This book is simply a tool to help you transition into your new role.

At the end of each chapter you will find some thought-provoking questions and a space for you to write about your own experiences. Don't be intimidated as you record your thoughts and feelings about motherhood or underestimate the importance of doing so. Motherhood is more than a process of helping your child grow. It is also a process of your own growth as a woman. After a few years have gone by, a record of both your child's and your own growth provides perspective on this never-ending adventure.

If you are giving this book as a gift to a new mom, there is a place at the end of the book for you to contribute your own advice as well. There's no better way to offer your support than to encourage a new mom.

CHAPTER I-

Enjoy Every Minute

As a new mom, I could be in line at the grocery store, or just out for a stroll, when friends and even perfect strangers were ready to offer this advice: "Enjoy this time with your baby." Most of the time I'd confidently smile and say that yes, I absolutely did love being a new mom. It was true. I did enjoy most days.

The "Other" Times

Then there were the other times—those days when I was more exhausted than I thought possible, I had dirty, tangled hair, and old, dried spit-up on my shirt.

Now I can laugh at our predicaments, but when my daughter, Kylan, was two months old, we faced a week so tough, terrible, messy, and downright miserable that most POWs would have rather sat in an enemy's camp for a week than move in with us. I am not kidding. I nearly had to wave the white flag of surrender.

"Yeah, right!" I thought. "How can I enjoy this time when my baby isn't sleeping, or when she cries all the time from gas pains or when she poops all the time and I feel like I just can't change *one more* diaper?"

Step Back and Look at the Positives

When you are in the midst of sleepless nights, frustration, and uncertainty, it may seem practically impossible to "enjoy this time with your baby." Yet, it is when things are the most trying, that it is critical to take a deep breath and remember that this precious person is a gift. Refocus your energy toward helping your little one adjust to his new world. Your baby would be lost without you.

It was frustrating for me to get up in the middle of the night to feed or soothe my baby because I was just so tired. But I realized if I only looked forward to the day that she would sleep through the night, I would have missed out on fully experiencing that precious stage of her life. Focusing on this fact helped me enjoy quiet nights with my daughter.

The Time Does Go by Fast

Most experienced mothers will say that the first few years go by especially fast. Not until I did some relaxing of my own, due to my husband's encouragement, did I begin to realize how much truth there was in this constant flow of advice. It took me a little while to get there, but it all finally made sense.

How did I achieve baby bliss? I laid aside the daily grind and concentrated on Kylan and putting her needs first.

Put Aside the To-Do List for Now

Put aside some of the to-do items on your daily list of mommy chores. Why? Because you can. You are the mommy. You are in charge, and furthermore, you can return to your to-do's in time.

You are not a desperate housewife, so surrender the urge to compare the cleanliness of your home to Bree Van de Kamp's. Close the door on the Donna Reed 1950's perfect-home mentality and trade it for the joy of daily, active game-playing, cuddling, story time, and parenting. House chores can wait—there will always be more laundry to wash and fold, tables to dust and dishes to clean. Furthermore, put the volunteering on hold and community events aside for a little while. *Babies don't stay babies for very long.* All of that stuff will be there later, but your baby won't.

At first, this was the hardest thing for me to do. I love a clean house. I like things in their place. So for me to let go of that for a season to be with my new baby was hard, but I can say without hesitation that it was one of the best choices I ever made.

If you're like me and can't stand to have a dirty house, either hire someone to help you or ask friends and family members if they would be willing to help out.

Take Five Minutes a Day

Finding space to step back and reflect on your new life with your baby can be done and can help you cherish the time even more. Taking five minutes a day to think about all the amazing new experiences you had that day can make a huge difference in your outlook. Did your baby move in a new way today? Mimic your funny faces? Sit up? Laugh?

Keep a journal and write a couple of thoughts in it each day or call a friend and share the highlights—whatever works best for you. Find a ritual that helps you pause and be mindful of your new life and the life of your baby.

A Privilege and an Honor

Never forget that being a mom is truly a privilege and an honor. Think about the profound gift you have received—you have been entrusted with another human being.

WHAT OTHER MOMS HAVE TO SAY:

When one of my kids is telling me a story, I try to put down what I am doing and really listen. I look at the way their mouth forms the words; I listen to the sound of their voice and the way that they say their words; I watch their eyes light up with enthusiasm; and I notice how they use their hands to help explain the story. When I take note of all these things, I get a big smile on my face…Kids really are so animated and funny.

ELIZABETH HEDDEN
MOM OF THREE GIRLS: AVERY, KATHERINE AND WHITNEY

Enjoy every minute because it flies by!

Angela Tuininga
mom of two: Benjamin and Leah

Enjoy every moment with your baby. Sometimes it may take a while to really figure your baby out, but the truth is most of the time the "mom hormones" kick in as soon as you hold your child, and you instinctively know just what to do. It will be you who can read his facial expressions, or identify and interpret the noises he makes. The first few weeks will fly, I can tell you that. So try to enjoy it!

CHRISSI HELLE
MOM OF TWO GIRLS AND ONE BOY

I had a dear friend who walked with me two days a week while we pushed our newborn babies in the strollers or bounced them in our baby carriers. We'd talk for hours about everything–it was so wonderful and important to have my fears and frustrations normalized by another new mom. Enjoy this time now because as your baby grows they suddenly want to run and not be confined in a stroller anymore which requires more of your attention. I wish I had appreciated this stage more than I did!

Anne-Marie
mother of two boys

I had always felt this huge responsibility to teach my kids all the life lessons they would need. What I've discovered as a mom, though, is that they are the real teachers. As long as I take the time to stop, listen and take in what they are showing me, the lessons are invaluable. I've learned more from each of them than I could have ever imagined.

Amy Beaudette,
Keaton, Abbie and Brody's mother

Get a digital camera and take tons of pictures. Don't worry about organizing them or getting them into a baby book, just take them and store them in some place safe. You hear people say it all the time, but it's true—they change so fast!

Sarah Donaldson
Colin's mother

My earliest memories as a new mom are feeding my daughter early in the morning while listening to the birds and crickets and just enjoying that quiet time with her. It's such a short time. I learned to enjoy that with my second child so much more because I knew the time would pass by so fast.

Dana McCoy
Emma and Ethan's mother

The time that your child is a baby goes by so quickly yet new mothers often feel like they have to keep up with their old work load. We end up stressed out and miserable. Play with your child. Put on a funny hat and giggle with your toddler or roll on the floor with your baby. The other stuff can wait, your baby will not. That's what parents miss when they are older....the joy of having a baby and playing with them. Soak it up. Soon, play time will be replaced with sports schedules and school activities. So play!

SARAH FULLER
HANNAH, GRACE AND JACK'S MOTHER

The important thing is to bond with your baby. Spend as much time with her as you can. They grow so much and so fast. Enjoy all the moments you can with your newborn because before you know it, she's rolling over, then crawling, then walking, then talking. My kids just started pre-school and kindergarten and I can't believe how quickly the time has gone by.

Chrissi Helle
mom of two girls and one boy

The time that you spend rocking your baby at 3am won't last. While it does, enjoy it. At first it seems like it really sucks to lose so much sleep night after night. But the moment you choose to walk into his nursery at the crack of dawn with an attitude of joy, life changes. This is the only time in your baby's life that you will get this chance to hold him, rock him, and love on him in the quiet and silence of the night. Choose to enjoy it.

McKinna Murnane
adoptive mother to Leeland
and birth mother to Bridgman

One thing I am constantly working on is slowing down and moving at my kids' pace. I tend to be in a hurry a lot and there really is not a good reason for it.

Elizabeth Hedden
mom of three girls: Avery, Katherine and Whitney

Pregnancy is the longest nine months of your life. I would encourage any first timer to really accept that, and to begin enjoying it as much as possible. You'll have a lifetime with your child, but only nine precious months of carrying and protecting that life in your own body. I always felt like I was never alone when I was pregnant. I talked to both my daughters as often as possible. I even began praying out loud nightly so they could hear my voice in prayer. It is a special time that not everyone will get to experience, so enjoy it to the fullest.

VERONICA CARGO
MOM OF TWO GIRLS: LILY AND JASMINE

I read recently that children laugh at least 400 times per day. As adults, we only laugh 15 times per day on average. For my girls, I want to try my hardest to ensure that they laugh a lot each day and stay kids for as long as possible.

Elizabeth Hedden
mom of three girls: Avery, Katherine and Whitney

My kids are still young enough that if Mom is happy, present and loving towards them, it doesn't matter what's going on, where they are or how many changes are happening—they just go with the flow! I really try to take time out to show them, no matter how busy things are, that they are the priority in my life!

Daniela Riley
mom to Will and Susana

Relax; you're actually going to be fine. You and your child will be okay. You might not believe it now, but you will. And I promise if you relax with your baby, your baby will be relaxed! Your baby knows only what he learns from you; if you teach stress, he will learn how to express feelings of stress.

McKinna Murnane
adoptive mother to Leeland
and birth mother to Bridgman

QUESTIONS:

What can you do to more fully enjoy your time with your baby?

What activities do you enjoy that you and your baby can do together?

What things are you okay with not getting done so you can spend more time with your baby?

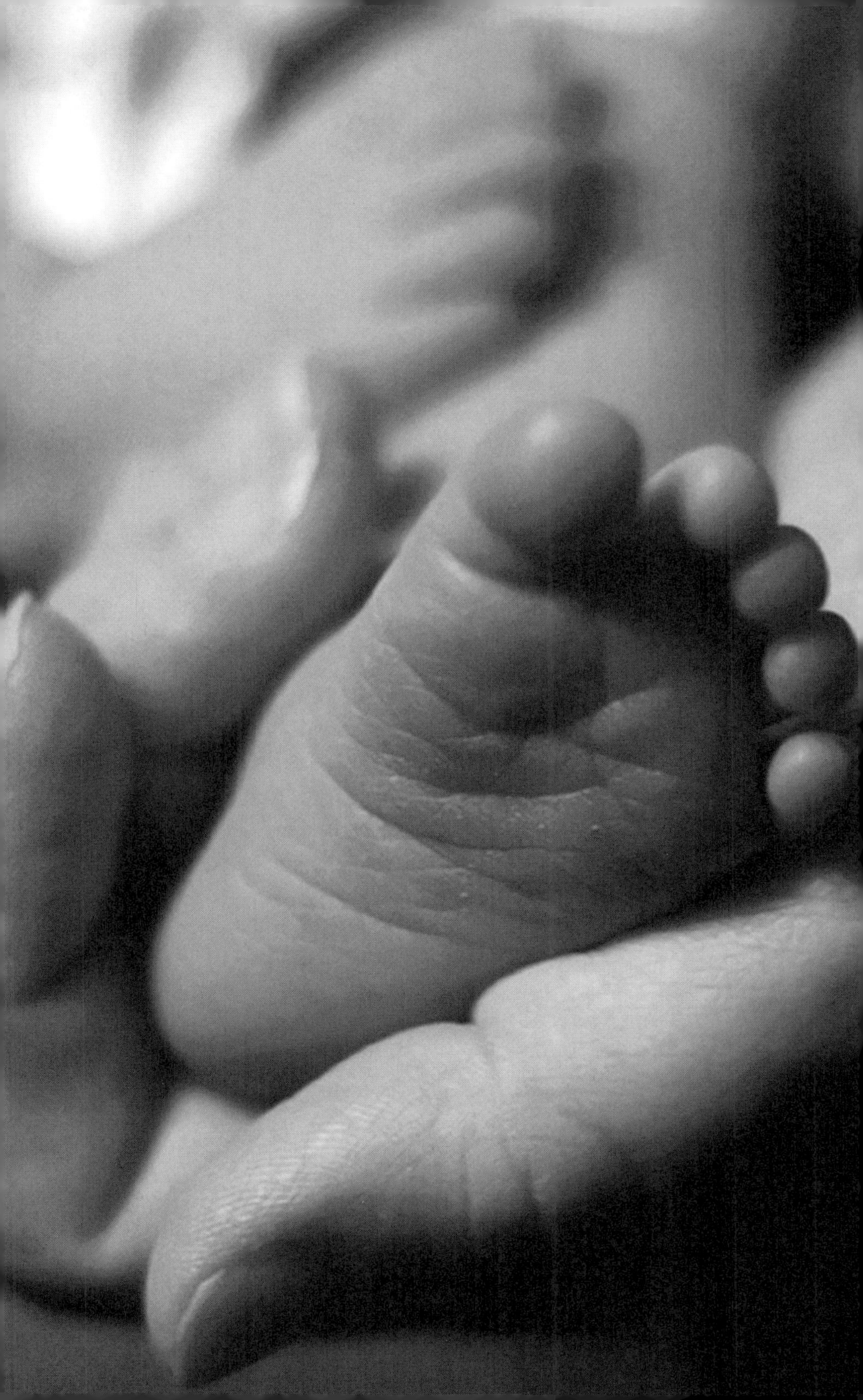

CHAPTER 2-

Fear Not, You Will Get a Full Night's Rest Again!

At the risk of sounding painfully obvious, *sleeping* is a huge part of your newborn's life. After all, it's one of only three things babies do during those first few months — eat, sleep and poop, right?

At first, I struggled to get my baby to sleep, especially during the designated nap times. She would be tired and fussy, and even though she was dry and well fed, she simply could not fall asleep. I had always heard that "sleep time is grow time" and that a baby could never get *too* much sleep. I also learned that I actually had to teach Kylan how to sleep. Knowing these things was very helpful to me, especially on days when it seemed all I did was work on getting her to sleep. Understanding that she wasn't being rebellious or stubborn but rather she needed her mother to teach her, gave me a new and patient perspective.

Call Someone for Help

Don't let your pride get in the way of asking for help. I sometimes feel that as Kylan's mom I should instinctively know everything she needs. However, I've come to realize that all moms have times of being completely perplexed by how to raise their children. Letting go of my pride has made a dramatic difference in my mothering. More than once, a desperate phone call to a friend has resulted in a new idea that drastically helped my situation.

Don't hesitate to call an experienced mother friend for advice.

Sleeping Schedule or Not?

Every child and every household is unique. While most babies benefit from developing a sleep schedule, the method of the schedule will look different for each baby. My husband and I learned how to put our baby on a schedule after reading, *On Becoming Babywise* by Gary Ezzo. When it comes to people's reaction to this book, it seems there is no middle ground. Every mom I know who has read it either *loved* it or *hated* it.

I loved it. I have one caveat though: I did not follow the book's method religiously. I was flexible on some things and modified a few others. I found that I didn't have to follow the instructions to the letter in order to get good results.

I'll be honest and say that despite our success with a schedule, during the early months of my daughter's life I was definitely more stressed about keeping her on it than I should have been. Just ask the moms whom I called practically every day. I have a sneaking suspicion that when they saw my name on the caller I.D. they groaned and let it go to voicemail. Remember, real life will always look different than it does inside a book. Don't stress if your child doesn't exactly follow the method you choose.

Five Quick Tips to Help Your Baby Sleep

Below are five quick sleeping tips that worked well for me. Keep in mind that what worked for me may not work for you. Sometimes it's just nice to have suggestions for different things to try.

First, always have your baby wear socks when he sleeps, both at night and when napping. My baby slept so much better when she had socks on.

Second, use a white noise machine; it quickly became my lifesaver. The minute I turned it on, my baby fell right to sleep.

Third, swaddle your baby while he sleeps.

Fourth, use a sleep aid. Mine was a homemade floppy rabbit that went along with the children's book *Guess How Much I Love You.*

Fifth, and finally, keep the room as dark as possible, even during naps throughout the day, if possible.

WHAT OTHER MOMS HAVE TO SAY:

A white noise machine works like magic!

ANGELA TUININGA
MOM OF TWO: BENJAMIN AND LEAH

One thing that really helped me was a regular schedule at night. I put my kids down between 7 pm and 8 pm, and they slept for a good 12 to 14 hours.

Don't be tempted to put your kids down later to get them to sleep longer in the morning. For whatever reason, that does not work. In fact, it's the opposite. When I had a night when I had to put the kids to bed late, it never failed that they'd wake up early the next morning.

Chrissi Helle
mom of two girls and one boy

Sleep when you can. Don't hesitate to nap when your baby naps. Everything is so much more manageable when you have had enough rest.

Mandy Phillips
Eli and Josie's mother

When Ben was about six months old, he started waking up in the middle of the night for no reason. He was not hungry, and he didn't need to be changed. My husband and I decided that we would let him cry it out, and not go into his room. This was very difficult for a few nights, but it eventually taught him to self-soothe and he soon became a great sleeper. Within a week he was fussing very little during the night, and he learned how to put himself back to sleep rather quickly. Eventually, if he did awaken in the middle of the night and cried for more than a minute, we knew something else was wrong, and we would tend to him at that time. We swore by the book *Good Night, Sleep Tight* by Kim West, which recommends putting your baby to bed sleepy but still awake. This book helped make bedtime very smooth for us.

Angela Tuininga
mom of two: Benjamin and Leah

Get your child on a schedule and sleeping through the night as soon as possible! No sleep means an irritable and discontented baby and an irritable mommy. A contented baby makes for a happy mom and a peaceful home!

Lindsey Hoelter
mom of two kids: Theron and Ainslie

It is okay for your baby to cry herself to sleep. It usually doesn't take very long before a baby will eventually go to bed without a fuss. I'm not talking about a sick child or child in pain. And I'm not talking about letting your child cry for hours and hours. But if everything is all right and you put your child down and she talks for a while or even cries, it's okay. You are not a bad mom.

CHRISSI HELLE
MOM OF TWO GIRLS AND ONE BOY

My daughter sleeps very well and we attribute that to routine and white noise. She sleeps well, even when we travel, as long as she has her blankie, paci and her noise machine. It's not easy to listen to a crying baby, but after the age of three to four months a pattern is established and you can set a routine.

Melissa Jantzen
mom of Ada and Will

There is way too much hype surrounding the "method" of feeding and sleeping. So many books…and each one claims their way is the best way. I believe each child is unique, just as each adult is unique. We don't develop our personalities when we grow up; we have them right from birth. I have seen this in both of my babies, and in the babies of my friends and my sisters, too. What works well for one does not necessarily work well for all.

I had so much pressure on me when my babies were little to follow the *Babywise* method. It promises so many amazing results, and yet when I tried the method my kids cried constantly–often to the point of not breathing and throwing up. Everything in me said "this is so wrong," but everyone kept telling me that was the way to do it. They said to give it more time.

I found that when I made the decision to do what felt right to me as far as when my children ate, how they went to sleep and even how often they went to sleep, I found great peace. The inner struggle that had plagued me for so long disappeared. My kids calmed down and were easier to manage–they were happier and slept better, which meant my husband was happier, too. It was quiet and peaceful in the house again.

I loved rocking my kids to sleep. I loved sleeping with them sometimes. I know moms that have taken many different approaches other than *Babywise* and none of their kids have problems due to not being fed or put to bed "correctly."

Motherhood is about making sure your children know they are loved, happy and healthy.

ROBIN SCHWARZ
MOM OF TWO KIDS: BRANDON AND KAYLEE

We put Ben to bed with a special "blankie" tucked under his arm every night long before he cared about having it, and the blanket quickly turned into his comfort item, which worked like magic when he was upset. We only give it to him when he sleeps, is hurt, or is in a stressful environment (doctor visits, new sitter, etc.). That way, he's comforted by it but isn't dependent on it all the time.

Angela Tuininga
mom of two: Benjamin and Leah

I am telling you, no matter how many times people tell you that you will lose sleep, you are never prepared. Lack of sleep is way worse than you can imagine!!

DIANA LIKES
EMORY AND FINN'S MOTHER

Don't underestimate getting your own sleep... they say you can never get enough and that's so true! Even right after you have the baby in the hospital let the nurse take your baby to the nursery so you can get some rest! I was the mom who let her kid sleep in the hospital room and now I wish I listened to the nurse when she said it's ok to request sleep!

Sharon Auw
Jaedyn Auw-Colman's mother

As hard as it is, you've got to let babies learn to settle themselves. Sometimes that may mean letting them cry for long periods of time. Once it's learned, the foundation for their sleep habits is formed for the rest of their life.

LINDSEY HOELTER
MOM OF TWO KIDS: THERON AND AINSLIE

Sometimes you just can't control naps because you are out and about during the day, but I have found that trying to keep bedtime a set time is good for both your kid and you. Make it a fun routine in the evening! About an hour before bedtime dive into the bath! Then after everyone is dried and jammied we read a book or watch a show together. Make it fun!

Daniela Riley
mom to Will and Susana

QUESTIONS:

Will you put your baby on a sleeping routine?
Why or why not?

When during your day can you take a nap?

Who can come over and watch your baby
so you can take a nap?

CHAPTER 3-

Bottle or Breast—Whichever Works for You Is Best

Even before I became pregnant, I planned on breast-feeding my baby when the time came. However, I told myself that I wasn't going to be one of those mothers that stressed over it if it didn't work for me. I would simply move to formula.

But something changed after Kylan was born. I guess a motherly instinct took over and breast-feeding seemed like the most natural and *only* right thing to do. It was something I did not expect.

Everything seemed fine during the first few attempts of breast-feeding. It appeared like Kylan was latching on fine, and the nurses at the hospital even praised me for having a good little sucker.

Then the Troubles Began

After a week of breast-feeding and thinking all was well, I took Kylan in for her one-week check-up and found that she was extremely jaundiced and had lost too much weight due to not getting enough food. The doctor immediately admitted her to the hospital.

I was devastated and couldn't believe this was happening. I had unknowingly been starving my baby; I felt like a failure as a mother. I thought breast-feeding a child was one of the most basic things a mother does. And I couldn't do it.

My baby was in the hospital for a couple of days getting a "sun tan" under the bilirubin lights. During that time the nurses worked with me on breast-feeding. I spent hours sitting shirtless with many nurses hovering over me, moving my breasts this way and that way. I wondered where my dignity had gone.

The Dreaded Machine

As I waited for my next training session to begin, a good-natured nurse rolled in a silver box and proceeded to attach a bunch of tubes and funnels to it. Handing me one of the funnels, she instructed me to press it against my breast. Then she flipped a switch and YOWZA! My nipple was being sucked away into a vacuum.

She left me to my misery.

As the machine yanked and pulled at my nipple, I briefly wondered if it was worth all the pain. At first, no milk came out. Then after ten minutes or so, we had a few drops of something—only it wasn't milk. My husband, who doesn't do well with the sight of blood, ran to get a nurse.

The nurse said that bleeding can be normal for some people and not to worry about it. After a few more minutes with the relentless suction machine, we finally had a drop of milk. Hallelujah! If I hadn't been half-naked and practically in tears, I would have told my husband to grab a camera.

Time to Supplement

Because my milk supply was so low, my doctor told me I would have to supplement with formula until my milk came in fully and the baby could get enough food from me. I was okay with using formula for a short time, but I was determined not to give up on breast-feeding. Because I was so determined, the doctor even suggested that when I fed Kylan, I run a mini tube that pumped out formula alongside my breast so she would think she was getting the milk from me.

Because I had a low milk supply, I needed to track how much

milk I was producing. I bought a very expensive breast pump. After pumping every two hours for several days, I was completely burned out and emotionally spent. Not only was I exhausted, but my breasts were so sore that I literally cried every time I had to pump. And even though I was pumping every two hours, I was only getting about 4 ounces of milk a day—not nearly enough to sustain a baby.

I was determined to endure the pain and not give up no matter what. After all, it was the best thing for my baby, right?

Time to Surrender

I had never been so torn about anything. On one hand, I felt like I would be failing my daughter if I gave up, but on the other hand, I felt like I just couldn't do it anymore. I was puzzled by how challenging and emotional this situation was for me. After talking to several of my friends who had breast-fed, I was also surprised by how many of them admitted they had experienced problems with it too. Yet somehow they all made it work eventually. Why couldn't I?

I finally realized that my situation wasn't a catastrophe. I talked with several other moms, all of whom I greatly respect, and they told me they hadn't breast-fed any of their children, and their kids all turned out just fine. I was concerned about my little girl not getting the health benefits that breast-fed children receive, but even my pediatrician said that out of her five children, the ones she breast-fed the longest actually had the most health issues.

So I quit. Nothing catastrophic happened. Kylan was fine.

Two years later I found out my body was physically unable to produce enough milk to feed a baby. It was not possible. I realized I had wasted all that time and energy trying to fill an impossible expectation I had about being a good mother. I've learned since to abandon expectations and to instead live fully in the reality of life with Kylan.

What other Moms have to say:

Nursing does not come naturally, even though it seems like it should. Don't be afraid to seek counsel from a lactation nurse before starting and stopping. It is easy to get frustrated with nursing, but it is the best thing for your baby—so don't give up.

Lindsey Hoelter
mom of two kids: Theron and Ainslie

Before I had a baby, I thought that nursing was the most natural thing in the whole world. But it turned out to be extremely challenging for me. Since I didn't really read up on the subject beforehand, I didn't know what signs to look for and what I needed to be doing. My oldest ended up not gaining his birth weight back until he was about a month old. He was in the failure to thrive category because I wasn't producing enough milk. I consulted a lactation specialist and tried and tried, but I had a low milk supply. We ended up having to formula feed 100% of the time. That was so traumatic for me; I cried and cried because I wanted to nurse so badly. But once Joey started getting enough to eat, he was a completely different and happy baby.

Jaimie Schuster
Joseph and Madelyn's mother

If you don't end up breast-feeding and your husband is willing to help with the feeding, I would recommend something I call block sleeping. Since my husband is a late-night person and my bedtime was always early, it worked out great for us. Instead of having a couple hours here and there and struggling to get through the night, my husband took the 8 pm to 2 am shift, and I took the 2 am to 8 am shift. That way, we were each guaranteed a solid six hours of sleep. We didn't start this until our daughter was about four months old, but when we had our second we started it from the beginning and it was a breeze to get through. By three months of age, our second child was sleeping through the night and was used to his crib. We didn't have to co-sleep and adjust from a bassinet; it was a very easy transition. Block feeding was a jewel-of-a-plan for the McCoy household!

Dana McCoy
Emma and Ethan's mother

Do not demand feed! Demand feeding does not promote structure and stability, both of which a child needs in order to thrive.

LINDSEY HOELTER
MOM OF TWO KIDS: THERON AND AINSLIE

I think the most important thing is not to let other mothers make you feel inadequate if breast-feeding doesn't go well for you. My twin boys were in the NICU for a month, and during that time I pumped and took milk with me to the hospital. Since they were so tiny and needed very little, I was able to produce enough milk for them. Very soon after we brought them home, however, I was no longer able to make enough for both of them. Other moms kept telling me, "Oh, you'll be fine. Your body will always make enough for your baby. Just keep trying and eat well." That is the worst thing to say to a new mom of twins, who barely has time to eat and who knows precisely how much milk she is pumping and how much her babies are drinking! I clearly wasn't making enough. I just had to accept it, take medication to increase my production for as long as I could, and then accept that I was done and the babies would be fine on formula…

One thing I loved about pumping was knowing how much my babies were eating. This is especially important for preemies—our neonatologist gave us a formula for how much milk they needed. There's something empowering about knowing how much food your baby is getting, especially in the beginning when weight gain is of the utmost importance.

LISA GREEN
MOTHER OF TWIN BOYS AND A GIRL

As your baby gets older, making baby food is not hard! Don't be intimidated. You can make a batch, pour it into ice trays, freeze it, and thaw it as you need it. Your baby will get the purest ingredients at an economical cost to you.

Daniela Riley
mom to Will and Susana

Fortunately, breast-feeding came very easy to me. My daughter latched on right away and we never had any difficulties. Maybe that's because I had no idea what I was doing so I thought of it as a new adventure and nothing to stress out over.

MELISSA JANTZEN
MOM OF ADA AND WILL

It helped me to find out as much information on breastfeeding before our baby was born. So when our baby arrived, I already knew it was going to take time, patience and some pain at first. Once I got over the initial hump, I did not regret it. If nursing does not come easy, for you or your baby, I would encourage utilizing many of the resources available to help. Seek advice from a lactation consultant, your baby's doctor, a family member or friend, even a local store may have experts available to assist you and baby. Keep in mind, some of the best and most rewarding things in life take the most work, but it is worth it!

Kendy Konecky
Gabbi and Kylie's mom

There were times when I was breast-feeding that I did not want to nurse for one reason or another, so I fed my baby warm goat's milk. It is possible for breast feeding mothers who do not wish to use formula to use goat's milk as an acceptable alternative as long as it is understood that it is not a replacement.

Jen Fischer
Beatrice and Norah's mother

QUESTIONS:

Will you breast-feed or formula-feed? Why?

If for some reason breast-feeding doesn't work out for you, how will you respond to the criticism you may inevitably receive from well-meaning friends and family?

Where can you go to get help from a lactation specialist if you need it?

CHAPTER 4-

Don't Be So Hard on Yourself

Life as a new mom is hard enough without putting pressure on yourself to be perfect. Becoming a new mom is a very challenging time. Recognize that it is also a time for treating yourself more gently.

You're a good mom. It's true. Don't doubt it. You are doing a wonderful job, so don't be hard on yourself. Furthermore, there's no such thing as a perfect mom. So let go of any unrealistic expectations and just do the best you can.

Don't Stress About What Doesn't Work

Foregoing breast-feeding turned out to be the best thing for me *and* Kylan. Rather than stressing over something my body would not do, I let go and was able to enjoy her even more. The decision to bottle-feed also gave my husband a chance to enjoy the feeding/cuddling time with her. It also allowed our daughter to bond with both parents right from the start. And besides that, my breasts were able to heal.

That was only the first of many situations as a parent in which I had to practice flexibility and learn to give myself some grace.

It *Is* a Big Change

Becoming a new mom is a huge change. If you have times when you resent the impact that having a new baby has on your life, you are not alone. Share your feelings with close family and friends. Talk openly with other moms and most likely you will find that they have similar stories and feelings.

I know there were times that I didn't enjoy the fact that so many of the freedoms I had taken for granted (like sleeping in) were no longer available to me. I didn't always enjoy times when I had to give up what I wanted to do in order for Kylan to get what she needed. However, I came to understand that these feelings are normal, and I also know I am not a bad parent if I feel this way at times.

What other Moms have to say:

Whatever path you chose for your family, whether it was naturalistic— homemade baby foods, cloth diapers, breast-feeding until age two—or more mainstream, the reality of your situation will dictate the choices you make for baby. Forgive yourself for whatever compromises you have to make to maintain your sanity. As long as you love your baby unconditionally, she will turn out just fine.

Jen Fischer
Beatrice and Norah's mother

Being a single mom of three kids isn't always easy. Sometimes it's hard to stay strong and calm not knowing what the future holds for me and my children. I have to put my strength in God to help me get through those troubled times. Philippians 3:13 says, "Let go of what lies behind and press on to what lies ahead." I continue to believe in myself and I always try to let my kids know that I love them more than anything else no matter what lies ahead. They know that this is true.

Luisa Prior
Hollie, Nathan and Jordan's mom

Please know that there can be moments that you want to cry, throw things or just get away from it all. That does not make you a bad person or mom. This means that its time for a mommy "time-out." I had a daughter that cried for the first six months of her life. I was lost and didn't know what to do. Thank goodness I have a supportive husband and family who encouraged me to put her down and walk away in moments of high stress.

JULIE HONAN
EVAN AND AVERY'S MOTHER

If you care enough to read a book about being a good mom, you're probably doing better than you think you are. Don't try to be perfect. Your mom wasn't perfect and you won't be, either. Besides, how boring would that be?

LAURA FALIN
MOTHER OF FOUR

When I first became a mom, I felt so overwhelmed by all the ways my life had changed—not so much with the baby stuff, but more with my changing relationships with my friends and co-workers, my husband, and my life in general…I just didn't feel normal. My mom told me that what I was doing was just a different kind of normal and soon I would find my "new normal." Somehow, that really helped me. Eventually you do start to feel like a regular person again. Getting ready to go doesn't take two hours anymore; you know how to pack a diaper bag and understand when not to take the baby with you. I don't know how it happens, but one day you just feel comfortable with your new life—with your "new normal"—and everything falls into place.

Sara Holmes
mother of two girls

You can have goals but never say "never". I said I would never let my baby sleep in our bed, then Bo slept with us until he was eight months old! If you don't live up to your expectations, you can't enjoy the experience as much, like having a little snuggler with you all night.

STEPHANIE JENNINGS
BO AND CARMEN'S MOTHER

Whatever your ideas and wishes and plans and ideals are, please be prepared for the fact that things might go differently. For example, I wanted the births of my children to be as natural as possible. But that didn't work out for either of my births. If your child's birth doesn't go exactly as planned, that doesn't mean you failed. I know of women who never seemed to bond well with her children because their supposedly perfect birth didn't go the way they had planned it. So don't allow what you think "should be" to ruin how it really happens.

CHRISSI HELLE
MOM OF TWO GIRLS AND ONE BOY

With both my daughters, the first month of their lives was overwhelming. I don't think there's a universal way to get past it, but I'm sure just knowing that other moms feel the same way offers a lot of comfort. I remember the first time I got out of the house after my first daughter was born. She was only a week old, and I walked to the store with my mom. It felt so good to get away—until someone asked me how far along I was. I was crushed as I realized what terrible shape my body was in. I don't think I left the house again until my daughter's six-week check-up. Your emotions do run wild those first few months. Understanding that helps tremendously. Surrounding yourself with supportive family and friends is really the only way to get through it. That and prayer...lots of prayer.

VERONICA CARGO
MOM OF TWO GIRLS: LILY AND JASMINE

I want new moms to know that we all feel guilty no matter what choices we make. Whether we use organic cloth diapers, nurse, buy only wooden toys…we will inevitably feel guilty about some decision or another and wonder if we have ruined our precious baby. It's called "mom guilt." And though you may escape it while your baby coos at you, at some point it will hit you. So, do not be surprised when it does. Some even experience it from the beginning when their "natural birth plan" turns into a C-section or their milk doesn't come in and they have to use formula. Whenever it happens, all mothers at some point come to the realization that they are not perfect. It happened to me more than once…

The most memorable was when my perfect little two-year-old decided to have a tantrum right in the middle of a crowded mall during a live children's performance. Not just screaming, mind you, but kicking and writhing on the floor! She had never done anything like that before. It was then I realized that I was no better than all those moms I had seen threaten their children in Wal-Mart. I no longer think or pretend that I am a perfect mother. Becoming a parent has been the most humbling experience of my life.

Sarah Fuller
Hannah, Grace and Jack's mother

I have learned that I am an impatient person, but I've also learned how to forgive myself and how beautiful is the verse "His mercies are new every morning, great is His faithfulness!" I've learned how important prayer is and how to trust God with their little souls (still learning that one).

Amy Bowman
mom of three girls: Teagan, Colsie and Avery

I have two boys, and no one told me to cover them when changing their diaper. The first time I changed Kemper's diaper at home solo he urinated all over me. Then the next time he was so sweet lying on the changing table, but when I took the diaper off, he urinated in his own mouth! I freaked out and that made him cry. As I was packing his things, thinking I was going to have to take him to the emergency room, I called the emergency care number and told them what had just happened. The sweet nurse just laughed and said, "It happens to the best of 'em"—and don't worry too much because urine is sterile!"

Donley Hicks
mom of two boys: Kemper and Pierce

If your baby has been sleeping and eating at fairly regular intervals and all of a sudden wants to nurse constantly day and night, baby is most likely in a growth spurt. It can be very frustrating when you think you've got a routine and it is suddenly disrupted. If you take the time to feed your baby on cue and do some extra snuggling, your milk supply will increase to meet baby's needs. Soon your baby will be back to a more normal routine. Make sure to eat and drink and get lots of rest yourself during your baby's growth spurt to keep your energy up.

Amy McKenna
Sophia, Cassidy and Leo's mother

As a new mom, you need to learn to give grace to yourself. This is your child, the one you have dreamed about your entire life. However, this child is still a bit of a stranger during the first few weeks. While you have felt this little one kick and move, and sometimes hiccough, you still do not know exactly how she likes to be held, or how she wants to interact with you. This is a relationship, a very special and unique relationship. Like all relationships, you must take time to learn about each other. Allow yourself this time and try not to let frustrations hinder this special time of wonder between the two of you.

JUDY DANIELL
MOM OF THREE BOYS: ISAIAH, CALEB AND NATHAN

QUESTIONS:

What things do you absolutely plan to do once your baby is here?

How will you take it if those things don't go exactly as you planned?

In what areas do you need to give yourself a bit of a break and not be so hard on yourself? Why do you think you are so critical of yourself in those particular areas?

CHAPTER 5-

Advice Is Nice—But Maternal Instincts Are Better

As a new mom, you'll get a lot of advice. Here's my advice on that: Do what works for you because you know your baby best.

It is a bit ironic to include this piece of advice in a book of advice for new moms. But, it is great advice.

Gather as Much Advice as You Want—Then Make Your Own Decision

It's great to get as much advice as you want or need from many different sources, but ultimately, no amount of advice can cover the multitude of situations you will face as a new mom. Once you feel you have enough information to make an informed decision, then follow your heart and do what you think is best for you and your baby. And once you've made your decision, don't worry about what other people say or do.

My Run-in with Unsolicited Advice

While I often felt clueless in my unfamiliar new role of "mom," I tried not to broadcast my insecurities to the world. And yet, the unsolicited advice was never-ending.

Shortly after giving birth I ran into an acquaintance in the grocery store. I did not know her well, but she was a very nice person and had a daughter about Kylan's age.

I fully anticipated most of the questions people asked me as a new mom. What is her name? How old is she? How much did she weigh at birth? How are you feeling? Other questions, I did not expect. And hers was one of them.

Her first question to me was if I was breast-feeding or not. Initially I thought it was an odd question coming from someone I hardly knew, but as a first-time mom, what did I know about normal new-mom questions?

Overall, I have to admit, I was surprised by how interested other moms seemed to be in whether I was breast or bottle-feeding my baby.

I started to explain that I had tried to breast-feed, but it didn't work for me, and before I could explain further, she interrupted and launched into a diatribe about all the benefits my child would be missing if I didn't breast-feed. Intellectually I already knew everything she said. I even personally agreed that "breast is best," but because of the toll it took on my body, both physically and emotionally, I just couldn't do it.

I knew if I started to explain my situation, it would turn into a long discussion. Frankly, I didn't want to revisit it again in a grocery store with someone I didn't know.

All I could do was smile and get out of that uncomfortable situation as quickly as possible. Since I wasn't prepared for her question, I wasn't sure how to handle it.

Second-Guessing Your Decision

Unsolicited advice can sometimes unknowingly lead to doubt. After that unfortunate interaction, I went home and started second-guessing my decision to formula-feed. I'd only been a mom for a couple of weeks and already I felt like I was screwing up.

I had to realize that my decision was the right one for me and my child. I had to decide that I was Kylan's mom and I really did know what was best for her. Accepting this freed me to become the mom I needed to be for my baby.

Do What's Best for You

Even if you don't ask for advice you'll still probably hear at least a dozen ways to help your baby sleep through the night, cure gas, and teach them to walk.

Most people mean well, even if they don't realize they are being insensitive to your feelings. When people have been through something hard, they want to share what they have learned in the hopes of helping someone else. Understanding that has helped me to extend grace to those dishing out the unsolicited advice.

Remember, however, the opposite is also true. If you like to offer your opinion, remember how it felt for you to receive unsolicited advice, and wait to give it until you are asked.

What to Do When This Happens to You?

If you are given advice from a stranger or a friend—or even your own mother—that you think is a bit wacky, don't waste your time debating or try to convince them otherwise. Just say, "Thanks for the tip," and then do whatever is best for you. Remember, you are the mom.

Do what works for you. You are the only one who knows your baby best.

What other Moms have to say:

Everybody has some child-rearing issue they feel passionately about—for example, breast-feeding, natural childbirth, or circumcision. It could be your mother or best friend that pushes the virtues of their pet cause. Whoever it is, just remember it is your baby and therefore you get to make your own mistakes. They had their own chance! My husband and I decided not to circumcise our son, and boy, did everybody have an opinion about it. Most thought we were weird, and I was surprised by how many people felt free to voice their opinion about what I thought was a private matter. Now I can't believe what a non-issue it is in his life. Nobody ridicules him. He doesn't have a complex. A decision that seemed at the time would make or break my son's psychological well-being doesn't even come into play. So politely listen to your mother or friends and then make up your own mind.

Sarah Fuller
Hannah, Grace and Jack's mother

My advice to new moms is to remember that you are the mom. It is amazing to me how bold other moms are in giving their advice and how quick they are to tell you that you are doing something wrong. As a first-time mother of twins, not only was I doing things wrong, but I was doing them wrong twice! I remember one time when an older mom not-so-politely informed me that my five-month-olds were not sleeping through the night because I wasn't feeding them enough. She said I needed to feed them more fruit (even though I had not been given the okay for baby food by their pediatrician yet).

I couldn't even get them to finish their bottles, and yet somehow I wasn't feeding them enough! Don't misunderstand me, though. Advice from other moms is invaluable and can be very helpful. However, take all advice with a grain of salt and see how it fits for you and your new baby. Don't feel bad if you don't do things exactly like your mother or mother-in-law or best friend did. You know your baby better than anyone else, and it is up to you to decide what is best for your family.

KELLY MCGRANAHAN
CLAY, LEVI, AVERY AND JUDAH'S MOTHER

My colleagues threw me a sweet baby shower. In place of the traditional cheesy shower game, everyone instead wrote a piece of advice on a strip of paper. When I got home, I eagerly read each and every strip, searching for all of the answers before my baby girl arrived. The very last strip I opened read, "Stop listening to everyone else's advice and trust your instincts." I found it amusingly ironic that this would be the last piece of advice I read. Once our precious girl arrived, I was constantly striving to be the perfect mother. I worried about her being too attached to her pacifier. I worried that she didn't eat enough. I obsessed over her sleeping schedule.

Would she ever nap on her own in her crib? Why couldn't I get her established into a sound sleeping routine during the day? I read books by the dozen and asked all of my mommy friends for their advice. Then one day it dawned on me. Why wasn't I taking the advice of my co-worker to stop listening to everyone else's advice and trust my instincts? Since then, I have been trying to just listen to my child's needs and trust my instincts. Not every theory works for every child. Not every program works for every parent. Trust your instincts! God gave them to you for a reason.

Jill Sinclair
McKenna and Keegan's mother

No matter what the books or experts said, I didn't follow other people's advice unless it felt right in my heart. I was told by my doctor to let Kyle cry it out at night to help him learn to fall asleep. I decided to follow my doctor's advice. So I put Kyle down in his crib for the night and he began to wail. I lay in my bed in tears. I hated to hear him cry, and it just felt wrong in my heart not to go to him. Finally, after an hour of crying I couldn't take it anymore. My heart told me this wasn't right. So I went in and rocked him to sleep. That became our routine. Every night I'd rock him to sleep. I loved rocking my baby to sleep and getting that one-on-one time. It became my favorite time of the day. Kyle eventually learned to fall asleep on his own, but I still rock him each night before he goes to bed and I love every moment of it. I followed my instincts and, in turn, have developed a special bond with my son—a mother's heart always knows best!

Lisa Kirchhoff
Kyle's mom

I read A LOT while I was pregnant and after my children were born. I became frustrated and confused with all the conflicting advice. I have since learned that reading for knowledge is extremely important, however not one book is going to provide exactly what you and your baby will need. All children are different, and its best to take bits and pieces from different sources that will suit your family best.

Julie Honan
Evan and Avery's mother

Trust your instincts as a mom. There are no guidebooks. You will get to know your baby, and your instincts will usually be right. Yes, doctors and more experienced parents can guide you, but you'll know what's best.

Jaimie Schuster
Joseph and Madelyn's mother

As a new mom, give grace to family and friends. Many people want to help you during this new time. Without overwhelming yourself, allow them to help. There are no prizes handed out for doing it all by yourself. In fact, when others help you, they give you renewed energy. Also, with new babies comes lots of advice. Some advice is wanted and some is not. Give them some grace when telling you things that are inappropriate or unnecessary and remember that they really just want to help.

Judy Daniell
mom of three boys: Isaiah, Caleb and Nathan

When my son, Nathan, was three years old, he swallowed a quarter. Don't ask me why. I have no idea. Was he craving metal? Maybe. Was he wondering what a quarter tasted like? Perhaps. Did it seem like a brilliant and imaginative idea at the time? I'm sure it did. Moments later, however, as we rushed to the emergency room, his idea had lost its brilliance entirely.

At the ER, we were told that the coin was stuck in his esophagus and would have to be surgically removed. They directed us immediately to the children's hospital, an hour away. By the time we reached the x-ray department of the children's hospital, the quarter had completed its journey down the esophagus and reached Nathan's stomach. All that was left to do was to watch the poop. Yes, you read that correctly, we had to watch the poop. Every day, every night, every poop. I became so effective at this task that, with plastic fork in hand, I could assess in nearly ten seconds flat whether or not the poop was loaded.

For a week I did this with no success. I called the doctor. "Give it a few more days," he told me. But after another week of poop patrol, still no quarter. The doctor didn't believe me. "I'm sure it passed, you probably just missed it," he assured me. Really? I'm combing through poop with a fork and I might have missed it? Well, he was "the doctor" and probably to prove me wrong in the meantime, he ordered an x-ray. The x-ray revealed the truth: a bright white circle in the middle of Nathan's stomach. Score one for the poop patrol! Two more weeks went by and I suspected my son was still twenty-five cents richer. Another x-ray was ordered to pacify my clearly irrational belief that the quarter had not passed. Lo and behold, the quarter lived on. Poop patrol two, rock-star doctor zero! Four weeks and thirty-seven plastic forks later, no quarter. More x-rays were ordered. X-rays that definitively and victoriously supported the poop patrol…

Finally, I requested another doctor. And finally, someone listened to me and treated me like the smart, perceptive, capable mother that I am. Perhaps the sweetest words I've ever heard went something like this, "It won't come out on its own." So on a lovely warm day in October a simple surgery was performed by the nice mother-loving doctor and the quarter was removed. And as we drove home with our less valuable son still groggy in the backseat, the head of the poop patrol had a sly, cocky smile on her face as she realized that mother's intuition had just had a stinky, but significant, victory!

KRISTINE HERRING
JOSHUA, NATHAN AND ELIZABETH'S MOTHER

Being around other moms is essential. They are a wealth of knowledge. I've gotten so many terrific ideas from other moms who are gifted in areas that I am not. They offer wonderful advice and are great sounding boards, too!

Lindsey Hoelter
mom of two kids: Theron and Ainslie

QUESTIONS:

How will you react if you are caught off guard by someone offering an unsolicited piece of advice?

If you are not accustomed to trusting your intuition, how will you learn to listen to your maternal instincts?

Whom do you appreciate and would seek advice from?

CHAPTER 6-

Let Go of Expectations—Being a Mom May or May Not Be What You Imagined...

Nobody ever told me how hard being a new mom could be. I'd always heard it would be challenging, but for me, the first three months were *more* than challenging.

Expectations Can Be Wrong

I guess I thought that caring for an infant would be easy. I thought my daughter, Kylan, would sleep when I wanted her to sleep, be happy when I wanted her to be happy, eat when I wanted her to eat, and so on. My expectations of what it would be like were totally off-base.

How to Have Realistic Expectations

To have realistic expectations means to never assume anything is going to be a certain way. And then, at the same time, completely assume that babies will need to eat and babies will need to sleep and, most importantly, babies will need to cry.

When things don't go the way you planned or thought they would, you will just have to learn how to roll with the punches.

We all have expectations of what life will be like when the baby arrives. Even if we think we don't, we do.

Babies Cry When They are Bored

I had a good friend tell me that babies, just like the rest of us, can (and do) get bored. The only way they can express boredom is by crying. Seriously. What else can they do?

By comparison, when we adults get bored, we might decide to do any number of things to alleviate our boredom, such as read a newspaper. Babies, on the other hand, can only cry. So she told me that when I have tried everything I can think of and nothing soothes my crying baby, maybe she's just bored. When I need help coping with the crying, I try to picture my daughter in glasses reading the newspaper. A funny thought, but very helpful.

Realistic Expectations about Your Body

Be realistic about how quickly or slowly your body will get back to feeling normal.

Even a year after giving birth, my body was not where I wanted it to be and some things about my body had permanently changed. Some moms lose the extra weight quickly, but for others, it can take some time. Even though my body had gone through incredible changes. I expected to return to normal much quicker than it did. It's amazing how many different kinds of changes your body goes through while you're pregnant. Your skin can change, your hair could change, and even your metabolism can be different.

I wasn't in the best of shape before I got pregnant. So as my body was going through the many changes of pregnancy, the weight gain was hard on my self-image.

Yet after Kylan was born, I always found an excuse or a reason not to exercise. Sometimes I was able to find something else to do around the house that needed to be done—like suddenly reorganizing the medicine cabinet or sweeping the kitchen floor.

I eventually learned that finding time to work out, even when you're busy and tired, is possible. Here are five easy things you can do to squeeze in a little work-out.

First, while you wait for the bottle to warm up, do a couple of chair dips, squats and sit-ups right in the kitchen.

Second, throw in a 15 to 30-minute exercise video while your baby is doing some tummy-time. Who knows, maybe he'll get a kick out of watching you jump up and down or do some crazy leg work.

Third, have a family member or a good friend come over for an hour or so while you run off to the gym. You might be surprised how energized you'll feel when you return home.

Fourth, jumping rope is a quick-and-easy workout that gets your heart going if you only have a few minutes.

And fifth, strap the little one into a stroller and head outside for a brisk walk in the sunshine. Queue up your iPod and you'll soon forget how tired you were.

You may not get back into shape as quickly as you would like, but just doing *some* exercise will help you start to feel a little more confident about getting your pre-baby body back.

WHAT OTHER MOMS HAVE TO SAY:

Once you think you've figured everything out, your child will move into a new stage of life. Expect and accept change; it's the only constant in your new life!

LINDSEY HOELTER
MOM OF TWO KIDS: THERON AND AINSLIE

Something was seriously wrong. I had just had my second child. He and I were deeply in love and strongly bonded. I even felt inexplicable joy when I held him. Yet I wasn't myself. I couldn't think straight, I couldn't organize my thoughts enough to do simple tasks, and most worrisome was that I cried. A lot. I cried all the time. My husband finally convinced me to see my doctor. I sat in her office and through ugly, hiccupy sobs, explained that I wasn't depressed. I thought that women with postpartum depression wanted to hurt their children and I was so in love with mine. My doctor explained that most often, postpartum depression has nothing to do with psychotic behavior. She explained that I had the perfect setup for such a problem.

We had just moved to a new city, I was isolated, and I had had a very difficult pregnancy. My doctor put me on a low dose antidepressant and within days, I was my old self. And while there was great relief and joy at feeling normal again, my shame was deep. I felt inadequate for needing drugs. I swore my husband to secrecy and didn't tell anyone for nearly a year. It wasn't until a friend opened up about her own struggles, that I found the courage to start talking about my own. I was shocked and relieved to find that many women had gone through similar situations. I realized that I wasn't alone, I wasn't a failure, and this didn't make me an inadequate mother.

SARA
MOM OF TWO

One thing my mom used to say that made me smile is "it's okay for the baby to cry a bit, it strengthens their lungs." It's true. It's okay for you to take a shower and let the baby fuss while you do so.

CHRISSI HELLE
MOM OF TWO GIRLS AND ONE BOY

It really took me by surprise how demanding having a child was, and how often I had to choose to put my children's needs before my wants. It surprised me how hard this was for me to do at times. My advice to new moms is to have realistic expectations—because I did not. I expected motherhood to be easy and come naturally since I had always adored kids and longed to be a mom. My fight with self took me by surprise. I wish I'd been close to a seasoned mom who could have told me that while being a mom is indeed a wonderful gift, it won't always be easy and will stretch you by requiring you to put your own needs, wants and desires aside. But also, that there would be many wonderful opportunities for growth along the way—and to look for those.

Amy Bowman
mom of three girls: Teagan, Colsie and Avery

When I had my second child, I didn't expect to be so frustrated! There were times when both of my kids were upset and cried at the same time. I've found that if I just stayed calm, I was more likely to get them under control quicker. I took a couple deep breaths, and then dealt with each one individually.

Daniela Riley
mom to Will and Susana

Try your hardest to clear your mind of all expectations of what it will be like to have a baby or even to give birth. You may or may not feel that amazing instant bond that many mothers talk about. You might feel like someone just dropped a total stranger on your chest. You might not "feel" very close, loving or bonded to the baby right away. Don't worry, it will come. It might take hours, days or months, but it will come.

As much as I didn't think I had big expectations of what having a baby would be like, they were still there. Even if you don't realize you have them, there are always expectations. Friends had talked about this amazing "moment" when they gave birth and how it was so euphoric and how they just couldn't wait to experience that feeling again...

When Jonah was born and I didn't feel anything like that, I felt guilty and wondered what I was missing. I just felt numb. I was tired and anxious, and I didn't have that amazing feeling that others had described. But, it came. It came in brief moments here and there…and then more and more frequently. Everyone's experience is different, and I think we lose sight of that.

Jenni Smith
Jonah, Lucy and Levi's mom

You may or may not have planned to have a baby, but here is what I found out very early on: Your attitude will mold your pregnancy, your birth experience, and ultimately the relationship you will have with your child. The thing that my husband and I heard so often before we had children is, wait as long as you can. Once you have children, your life will be over. You will be stuck at home, you won't sleep, you won't eat, and your social life will be down the drain. Frankly, it freaked me out a bit. I come from a big family, and it never seemed like life was "over" for my parents…

Our first pregnancy wasn't planned, but as soon as we found out we sat down and talked about the things that would change. And you know what? They were exciting things! I mean, yes, you don't sleep at first, and yes, your house will be a mess, and yes, your make-up and hair won't look tip-top all the time. But you have a little baby that you get to watch grow, and every day he or she will do something new. Life isn't over when you have kids; instead, you get a fuller, richer one.

CHRISSI HELLE
MOM OF TWO GIRLS AND ONE BOY

It's okay to let the baby cry. I remember this one day when my son Joey and I were just not getting along at all. I'd done everything I could; fed him, changed him, put him in his bouncy, walked with him. But all he did was cry and cry and cry. Some days are like that.

Jaimie Schuster
Joseph and Madelyn's mother

Be prepared…even though you have delivered a child, it will take at least four months to fit into your pre-pregnancy clothes. And even then, the stomach you were used to is well hidden by looser skin!

DIANA LIKES
EMORY AND FINN'S MOTHER

It's normal for babies to need 19 to 22 hours of sleep a day. Their bodies are growing so much in the first year. Sleep equals a contented baby! So don't be alarmed if you think they are sleeping too much.

Lindsey Hoelter
mom of two kids: Theron and Ainslie

QUESTIONS:

What expectations did you have about what parenting would be like?

After your baby was born, did you find your expectations to be realistic?

CHAPTER 7-

Heaven's Sake, Let Others Help You!

If family members or friends call and ask if they can help you after the baby arrives, your answer should always be yes!

Even if you are the type of person who doesn't like to ask for help, let others help anyway. The fact is, you have a lot going on and this is no time to try to be supermom. So even if you feel like you have everything under control, allow others to help you.

Make a List

When someone offers help, it can be hard to come up with something on the spur of the moment. Keep an ongoing list of things you would like to have done. Then when someone asks how they can help, you can refer to your list and give them options. This is better than saying the first thing that comes to mind—or worse, drawing a blank and saying nothing.

Your list might include anything from fixing a meal, to doing the dishes, to running to the grocery store, to making your bed or even doing a load of laundry. Many of these things people can do in conjunction with their own errands or chores. If a friend is making a trip to the grocery store to do her own shopping, it's really not that big of a deal for her to pick up a couple of items for you. So ask.

Most People Will Gladly Help

Most people are not only willing but *want* to help in any way they can. Do not feel guilty about accepting a helping hand. Undoubtedly you'll have an opportunity to return the favor for them someday.

And even if no one offers, there is no shame in asking for help. Sometimes people don't offer to help simply because they don't think about it. Many people even feel honored when someone confides in them and their need for help.

Let Go of "Your Way" and Allow Your Spouse to Help

Whether or not you have people lined up at the door to help you, let your spouse or significant other share the job of caring for your newborn.

I am very fortunate to have a husband who wants to be a part of the day-to-day care of our daughters. However, one thing that was hard for me was letting Nathan do things his own way. I had to let go of my tendency to remark on how he was burping her, or what he was feeding her for dinner. It wasn't that how he was doing it was wrong or hurting the baby, it was just that it wasn't the way I would have done it.

For example, after Kylan started eating solid food, we often fixed her chicken nuggets. I would cut each nugget up into six pieces, and Nathan would only cut it in two. I thought the two pieces were too big for her to handle, but she lived and probably never knew the difference. For some reason this was a big deal for me.

Another example is that I would always warm her vegetables up a little bit in the microwave, but Nathan would feed them to her cold, straight out of the refrigerator. As long as your baby is not being harmed, let your spouse do it his way. Don't end up being the only person capable of taking care of the baby.

Another big one for me was letting my husband figure out on his own how to soothe Kylan. As a mother, I always wanted to step in and take over because I felt like I knew the best and fastest way to calm her.

The best thing that came out of standing back was that Nathan found an even better way to soothe Kylan when she would wake up at night—it was by gently bouncing her and saying *shh, shh, shh* close to her ear. Daddy soon became the one who had to get up in the middle of the night to calm her because he was much better at it.

Find People Who Support You

It is important to have some sort of support group that will celebrate with you in the good times and to be there for you during the tough times.

Good support people can help you move from feeling isolated and confused to feeling connected and empowered. Supportive relationships can also help us grow and feel more secure. So make it a priority to find or create a community of mothers you can talk to, hang out with and call for advice or hands-on help.

What other Moms have to say:

I had to leave the room the first time my husband changed a diaper because I was sure he would do it "wrong," and I didn't want to nag. As long as the health and safety of the baby isn't in jeopardy, try to let things go! You don't want to be the only one able to take care of the baby—it's good for your husband/partner to be very involved and it's good for your sanity!

Laura Falin
mother of four

Accept help from anyone who offers!

Angela Tuininga
mom of two: Benjamin and Leah

Don't leave Daddy out! Let Daddy be a part of your baby's schedule whenever possible—let him change diapers, burp, and play with the baby. It is so good for both Daddy and baby.

MANDY PHILLIPS
ELI AND JOSIE'S MOTHER

If you have a husband or significant other, allow him to take part in all aspects of taking care of the baby. Try not to step in every time the baby is upset. We all learn how to soothe and care for a baby at our own pace, and later on you will want him to be able to take care of the baby without your intervention.

Jenni Smith
Jonah, Lucy and Levi's mom

My advice is to ask for advice. Parenting is a learning process, so it is important to let go of your ego and become a good student in order to figure out what works well for you and your little one. I think it is easy to assume you will instinctively know what is best for your baby. This may be true in some respects, but why not seek advice from others who have more experience? Read books, ask your mom questions, ask your friends for input, take a proactive stance toward caring for this precious gift that God has placed in your life.

Kendy Konecky
Gabbi and Kylie's mom

Don't forget your single girlfriends! These are the women who will beg you to let them come play with your precious child (for free!) so you can get an hour or so of breathing room. These friends will relish being the "cool aunts" and are absolute lifesavers in a time crunch. My girlfriends without kids come over once a week for dinner and *Grey's Anatomy* after Caroline goes to bed. I get to have some social time without hiring a sitter, and after the show, the girls go out on the town and I go to bed! Maintaining relationships with your single friends will help prevent you from getting stuck in full-time mommy mode.

MARY CADY BOLIN
MOTHER OF TWO GIRLS

The most traumatic thing I had to deal with as a new mom was returning to work full time. My employer offered me six weeks off, which I gladly accepted, but because I had just started a new career, I wasn't eligible for more time under the Family Medical Leave Act. When my newborn was only five and a half weeks old, my mother-in-law arrived from out-of-town. She was coming to stay with us and help out for the next six weeks. Let me tell you, when you are a hormonal new mother, the last thing you want is someone staying in your house, taking care of your child. That first night was really rough! I was in tears, my mother-in-law threatened to go home, and my husband was angry with me for not more graciously accepting his mother's kind offer to help out. No one understood! I thought, *This is my baby, and I should be the one caring for her…*

While my husband comforted my daughter and tried to soothe her to sleep, my mother-in-law and I talked through things. Fortunately, she was very understanding. She completely agreed that this was not the ideal situation. She let me cry, then stayed anyway. And let me tell you, at the end of the six weeks, I did not want her to leave! What a gift to not only know your child is being well cared for, but to come home from work to a clean house and dinner on the table. I could not have asked for a better caregiver.

DIANA LIKES
EMORY AND FINN'S MOTHER

Let go of your pride and accept all the physical help you can get. Mental help or advice, on the other hand, won't always be helpful. Anyone and everyone will try to give you advice on what to do with your baby. Figure out what you and your partner are comfortable with and make your own parenting decisions.

Lindsey Hoelter
mom of two kids: Theron and Ainslie

After my C-section of my second child, I couldn't walk, let alone take care of my family! So I had many friends that offered to watch my two-year-old son which was a big key in helping me bond with my new baby! I was freed up to dote on my new little one and recover myself while my son was getting the attention he needed.

Daniela Riley
mom to Will and Susana

My mom was, without question, more help to me than anyone else when my babies were born. I don't think anyone could do a better job of stepping in and doing what needs to be done without being told. Even our husbands can't do that for us because often they've had little experience with babies, so there's a steep learning curve for them. Also, since my babies were born so early, we weren't prepared for them at all. My friends took me shopping for the items I needed, they came to the NICU with me some days when my husband had a work obligation and couldn't make it, and they delivered a week's worth of meals once the babies came home from the hospital. Additionally, I have a Korean grandma who helps two days a week from 9-4. She cleans the house, does laundry, and helps me feed the babies. She is great about shooing me out of the house as soon as the babies are down for their morning nap; this gives me a little time to exercise and even run some errands, which is so hard to do with two infants in tow. I have it pretty good!

LISA GREEN
MOTHER OF TWIN BOYS AND A GIRL

When you have your first baby, it's hard to know what kind of help to ask for—so I took whatever was offered.

Meredith Trullinger
mother of two girls

As a new mom, give grace to your sweet hubby. For many men, their first meaningful experience with a baby is with their own child. He will figure out the rhythm of this new family in time, but allow him space to grow without deflating his sense of self-worth as a parent. Give him opportunities to dress the little one. If you are nursing, dads can sometimes feel unneeded, but he can help with diaper changes. Find ways for him to feel included.

Judy Daniell
mom of three boys: Isaiah, Caleb and Nathan

During the first few weeks of parenthood enlist as much help as you can. Your body will be recovering from childbirth, and you will be sleep deprived as well. If you need help (or even if you don't think you do), ask for it. Ask your partner, family, and friends. I've found what helped me most in those early weeks was when people brought meals for us. Dinnertime was baby's cranky time, so not having to cook was a blessing.

Amy McKenna
Sophia, Cassidy and Leo's mother

QUESTIONS:

What tasks or chores do you feel comfortable letting others do for you?

Whom do you know that you would feel comfortable asking for help when the time arises?

CHAPTER 8-

Get Up, Get Ready, and Get Out of the House

Just three short weeks after I gave birth, my husband and I packed up our new baby and all of our belongings and moved from Ludington, Michigan, to Nashville, Tennessee.

Big life changes never seem to happen just one at a time for me. Here I was in a strange, new state, with a brand-new baby, without family or friends nearby, and because my husband was going back to school full-time, I was going to be the sole financial supporter for our family, too. Any one of these changes alone would have been a lot to handle.

Thankfully, I owned my own business and worked from home, so my work and clients could follow me wherever I moved. But while I was adjusting to the move and preparing to go back to work after a maternity leave, I didn't think I had time to get involved in other outside-the-home activities. I was busy trying to get settled and figure out the new routine of caring for a baby and working full-time.

On the other hand I knew that I needed friends and a support group to help me through life as a new mom. I also wanted my daughter to have other children to interact with besides just once a week with her nursery playmates at church.

Give Yourself a Reason To Get Ready Each Day

For me, getting out of the house at least once a day is essential. Even if I just do something simple, it gives me a good excuse to get ready in the morning. It also beats staying in your pajamas and feeling sluggish all day. (Granted, that's fun to do, too, but just not every day.)

Don't fall for the myth that you have to stay inside with a newborn. A little fresh air is good for both of you. I try to give myself and Kylan some variety. Sometimes I would walk with my husband to class, and other times I wandered around Target to see what new thing I could find that I could not live without. We also purchased a membership to the zoo (which quickly paid for itself), and we enjoyed many days there, too.

But my absolute favorite part of the week was going to Storytime at the downtown Nashville Public Library. By going regularly each week, I connected with some really great new mom-friends.

Other Groups

Besides storytime at public libraries, there are many different mom groups you can join that can give you something to look forward to each week and a reason to get out of the house.

Joining just about any mom group can be beneficial to you. The options are endless. There are Bible study groups for moms, groups for kids to play together, professional moms groups, and even groups where you can volunteer your time to a worthy cause alongside others.

By being a part of a group like this you'll be able to get to know other women who share similar values and interests. And it provides an opportunity to hear the challenges and struggles of other moms, which can help you feel less alone.

WHAT OTHER MOMS HAVE TO SAY:

It's hard to get out of the house—do it anyway! Even if you spend half an hour getting ready and go out for ten minutes, it's good to occasionally have a reason to shower. Just like any other skill, it takes practice to get out of the house with a new baby, but it will get easier and easier.

LAURA FALIN
MOTHER OF FOUR

One summer our family took a trip to stay with relatives. We decided one evening to go out for dinner. We were looking forward to going out while the grandparents watched the kids. I went to take a shower and get ready. When I had just put conditioner in my hair my brother yelled through the bathroom door that my youngest, Sophie, had a problem. I unlocked the door and called her into the bathroom. Still crying, she held both arms up over her face. "What's wrong, Baby?" I asked.

Sobbing, she said, "Mommy, I got a Lego stuck up my nose!"

I shouted for Sophie's dad to come in and get her. I did a quick rinse and hurriedly put on some clothes. By this time Sophie was hysterical! We made her lie down on the ground and confirmed that she did have a small, round, red Lego stuck way up her right nostril…

We didn't know if we should go to the ER, Urgent Care, or try to pull it out ourselves. Sophie was screaming and inconsolable. So her dad, my brother and I tried to restrain her and tried to remove the Lego with tweezers. It was no use. Finally, we gave up, and Sophie began to calm down. We moved her to the bed and she decided to let Daddy try one more time before we had to go to the doctor. She did a great job staying calm, but again no luck. In fact, we probably shoved it even farther up, and now her nose was bleeding.

So we went to a place called Kid Doctor Urgent Care and paid a $25 co-pay, but the doctor said it was too high up and he didn't have the right tool to get it out. (To which I asked, Hello? You're a Child Urgent Care...aren't Legos up the nose a common problem?) They sent us to the ER.

We stopped on the way and got Sophie a milkshake. She was now the sweetest little thing and soaking up all the attention. When we got to the hospital, we checked in to the ER and talked to a very nice nurse, but by the look of things we were going be there half the night—so much for dinner out!

As we were all sitting around the waiting room we began to talk about what things we should've tried back at the house. I suggested holding a vacuum up to her nose. That led to the thought of a bulb syringe. Then my brother suggested a straw. So we had Sophie lie on our laps in the middle of the waiting room and her dad stuck the straw up her nose and sucked! After two attempts, *pop* the Lego was out! We all cheered. One of the nurses came up to us and said, "Wow, that was cool!"

We went out to celebrate and bought Sophie some ice cream. And the lady behind the counter at the ice cream store gave her a huge cup full of jelly beans (cause she was so cute and got a Lego stuck up her nose).
I saw many sides to my little girl that night: scared, tender, strong and beautiful.

MALIA TAYLOR
TAYLOR, CARTER, ETHAN AND SOPHIE'S MOTHER

Form your own circle of supportive, positive people that you can trust and call on even if it's just for an adult conversation.

Stephanie Jennings
Bo and Carmen's mother

I think the best advice I could give a new mom is to join a new-mom group. Here in Seattle we actually have a formal organization called PEPS (Program for Early Parent Support) that my son Colin and I joined when he was two weeks old. I have to say, it was the best thing I did while on maternity leave, and at times I think it saved me from going over the edge. It was a group of 11 new moms and their babies, and we would meet once a week for a few hours at a member's house. We would talk about everything related to being a new mom. It was so comforting to know that other people were going through the same things I was and that it was okay not to be perfectly happy 100% of the time. Whenever I find out that a friend is pregnant, I tell her she must sign up for PEPS.

Sarah Donaldson
Colin's mother

When my baby turned exactly two weeks old, my husband headed back to work; I didn't think it would be any big deal. I had been at home with her for two weeks and we were just finding our way together. I didn't feel particularly stressed out or depressed. However, when my husband's car pulled out of the driveway that morning I literally burst into tears. I even started to laugh at myself because I had no idea why I was crying. I called my sister because she has three little ones and I figured she would give me good advice. As I poured out my emotions, I realized I was feeling completely overwhelmed. I hadn't left the house in two weeks, was struggling with breast-feeding, my body was still sore and "foreign" feeling, and I felt like my entire life before the arrival of my baby had disappeared in one giant poof! Thank goodness my sister told me I needed to get out of the house. She said even if for just a short walk that leaving the house every day was totally necessary for my mental health.

She was absolutely right. Getting out truly changed my mood and perspective. Some days I'd go to Starbucks for a coffee and other days we'd just go for a nice long walk around the neighborhood. There is something about the action of leaving your house that makes you feel more normal and at ease. What's even funnier is one of my best friends had a baby just two months after me. She emailed me at the two-week point with almost the exact "meltdown" that I'd had. I went to see her the next day and said, "Let's go for a walk." I explained how getting out for a short period each day made a big difference in how I felt mentally. It made me a better mom to Janice and also kept her from becoming too sheltered. After five months I got better and better at leaving the house and finding the places and outings that work best for Janice and me.

PJ Palmer
Janice and Charlie's mother

My first baby went everywhere with me. She still does—she's my easy-going, easy-to-please kiddo. But with baby number two, it gets trickier. Drive-thrus become your best friend. I once ran five errands and never got out of the car—if only you could fax in your grocery store order and swing by and have them load up your trunk!

MEREDITH TRULLINGER
MOTHER OF TWO GIRLS

When my baby was only 15 months old, we moved to a new state away from family and friends. I felt very isolated and alone so I decided to join a few mom groups, toddler play classes and went to library story times in search of finding new friends and playmates for my son. Even though I enjoyed these groups, I found myself so frustrated because I could not hold down one conversation–The minute I started to talk, my toddler would run off or try to take another child's toy away–typical toddler behavior, but it was not helping me make friends! I eventually discovered mom groups that met in the evening or during the day that offered child care. It was wonderful! I was finally able to carry on a conversation and not chase, feed or respond to my child while doing so…

My advice is to get involved with a lot of different classes and organizations as a new mom and you will find several good friends. Go to a meeting or class at least several times before you judge the quality of the group. New moms are constantly cycling into these groups, so you may meet one of your best friends at the next meeting or playgroup. It takes time to develop new friendships, and it takes even longer when you only have short snippets of time for conversation.

Anne-Marie
mother of two boys

Getting out of the house was a must for me (and still is when I am home from work). The day after I came home from the hospital I hopped in the car at 7am and went straight to Starbucks. I have always been one that needs to get out and stretch my legs. Whether it's a ride in the car, a trip to the mall or the zoo or just a stroll around the block, a change of scenery is a must. Which leads me to something else...I think it is imperative to socialize your kids. It will make your life and your child's life so much easier and enjoyable. There is nothing better than hearing a stranger say, "Your baby is so happy."

MELISSA JANTZEN
MOM OF ADA AND WILL

Getting out of the house when she was first born was an adventure. What used to take five minutes—jumping in the car and going to the mall—now took all morning. It was a full day outing. We packed the bag, the bottles, the formula, the burp clothes, and planned out what time we would eat, play, and go to the bathroom. It was scary the first couple of times because you just did not know what to expect as routine for your child. Now with two, sometimes I don't even bring a diaper, and pray they don't poop or pee all over the place. I'm more relaxed with number two!

Dana McCoy
Emma and Ethan's mother

QUESTIONS:

What reliable support can you find when you need some mommy alone time?

What young moms do you know who can tell you about some of the local activities in which you could be involved?

CHAPTER 9-

When It Comes to You and Your Baby, There's No Comparison

When my friend's baby was sleeping through the night at the early age of eight weeks old, I thought to myself *I must be doing something wrong.* Here I was following the same method as my friend, and yet Kylan was almost nine weeks old and still waking up in the middle of the night. Since I knew that sleeping through the night at an early age was possible, I stressed over the fact that my daughter wasn't.

When it came to walking, however, my daughter did this much earlier than most. It's amazing how some kids are cruising around the living room by ten months of age, while others don't demonstrate that type of mobility until well after their first birthday.

Throughout Kylan's first year, I had to remind myself that babies can develop faster in some areas than others. And if you haven't noticed, babies don't pay much attention to developmental charts. They choose to reach milestones when they are good and ready to do so.

Milestones

Developmental milestones are a set of functional skills or age-specific tasks that most children can do at a certain age range. Your pediatrician uses these milestones to help check how your child is developing.

First-year milestones include fine motor skills such as picking up small objects, gross motor skills such as crawling or walking, language and responding to sounds, social development, and cognitive growth.

There is a wide range of normal. Some new moms panic the second their baby is late reaching a milestone. Every child is different, and therefore their growth rates and developmental speeds will vary greatly.

If your baby does something late, it doesn't mean that your child is behind or delayed. By the same token, if your baby is ahead of their peers in a certain area, it doesn't necessarily mean they are gifted either. Sorry.

While you should respect the developmental timetable, it's pointless to stress out or obsess about it. Instead, spend a little extra time on the things you want your child to learn and guide them to success as they learn it in their own time.

What other Moms have to say:

I had a friend with twins born just four months before mine, and I spent the first several months as a new mom comparing my twins to hers. I was so frustrated because my babies weren't following the same schedule as my friend's. I would look at her babies and think "OK, in four months my babies should be doing that." When it didn't happen, I would think I had done something wrong or wasn't a good enough mom. It wasn't until I accepted the fact that my babies were different from hers that I was able to relax and start to enjoy my kids.

Kelly McGranahan
Clay, Levi, Avery and Judah's mother

Resist the urge to compare yourself to women who aren't mothers. When I had my daughter, I was twenty-one, which meant that all of my friends were still in college, going out, sleeping as late as they wanted, and looking fabulous. All this time I was growing a belly, feeling more and more tired, and preparing to alter my social schedule—and the rest of my life—entirely. Comparing my situation to that of women who had completely different priorities proved unhealthy and unrealistic. Seek out other mothers with lifestyles to which you can more easily relate.

MARY CADY BOLIN
MOTHER OF TWO GIRLS

Competition is what drives us to achieve higher goals. Any parent who says they don't compare their kids with other kids is blowing smoke. Instill a positive competitive nature in your kids—it will help them through life…
but don't forget to let them know that winning isn't everything.

MEREDITH TRULLINGER
MOTHER OF TWO GIRLS

One of my favorite things about being a mother is seeing the differences in my children. I marvel at how different my kids are in spite of coming from the same set of genes. My oldest is quiet, silly, shy, afraid of new things, and an amazing reader. She is a girly-girl yet loves bugs and pleads for the life of a spider like it's Charlotte. She is very similar to her father. Both would prefer to sit quietly than try out a new carnival or something fun. My second is almost my clone. She thrives on adventure. She wants to tackle each new thing. She is an avid puzzle-person and does puzzles like a mad genius. She gets impatient about growing up and wishes she was already a grown-up. Both are beautiful—just in different ways. My third child rocked my world! He's the rough-and-tumble boy who throws a football like a pro. He's a charmer who can flash a smile and save his behind. Seeing how different and amazing each one is almost makes me want to keep having more just to see all the variety that can come from one set of parents. Almost.

Something hopeful for those with high-needs children to keep in mind is that just because you have one very challenging child, that doesn't mean they all will be. My first one had colic, but my second was the easiest baby there could be. They are all so different.

Sarah Fuller
Hannah, Grace and Jack's mother

Kemper is my oldest, and he was sleeping through the night at five weeks old because I followed the advice in a book called *On Becoming Babywise*. I never understood parents that couldn't get their children to sleep through the night, and I have to admit there were times when I was silently critical of them. But then my second came along and I followed the *Babywise* method just like before and yet I had a completely different outcome. At eight months of age, my baby was still not sleeping through the night!

Donley Hicks
mom of two boys: Kemper and Pierce

Be careful what you wish for. Our first son, Joshua, was a very early talker. He spoke his first word at nine months and shortly thereafter the floodgates of speech opened wide. When our second son, Nathan, came along, we fully expected a repeat performance. Much to our dismay, his first birthday came and went without so much as one word. Six months later there were a few one-syllable words in his repertoire, but nothing near Joshua's accomplished vocabulary at that age. We waited and wished, desperate for the child to express himself. We grew increasingly frustrated with his lack of communication and would encourage him over and over to "use his words." We worried about his hearing and wondered if we had somehow inadvertently contributed to his lack of speech.

Just about the time we were about to seek help on the matter, Nathan turned two and nearly overnight the dam broke. We were thrilled—well, mostly…One particular exchange right after he started talking made us long for the golden silence of previous days.

One morning, I found Nathan sitting beside the open pantry with boxes of cereal dumped out all around him. With a stern voice and a pointed finger, I began to reprimand him. I had barely gotten his name out of my mouth when he looked directly at me and said, clear as day, "Don't say no to me, okay?!"

Kristine Herring
Joshua, Nathan and Elizabeth's mother

Every child is so different in their abilities, growth, and personality that there's no point in comparing them. Unless your child is not reaching the developmental milestones within a reasonable time frame, then comparing your baby with others should not even be an option.

LINDSEY HOELTER
MOM OF TWO KIDS: THERON AND AINSLIE

Don't compare—just because your friend's baby was sleeping all night at four weeks doesn't mean yours will—or should. Don't put pressure on yourself or your baby to be like someone else.

MANDY PHILLIPS
ELI AND JOSIE'S MOTHER

I think comparing your child to others stems from an innocent desire to gauge whether your child is where they need to be and whether you are doing a good job as a parent. While it may be natural to compare your baby to other babies, it isn't necessarily healthy to do so. It also seems like it is the worst with your first kid. With my second child, I didn't feel the same kind of pressure to make sure she was perfectly "on schedule"—whatever that means! I really try to just encourage my kids but not pressure them to "move ahead" if they aren't ready. If you push them, it can end up having the opposite effect and delay them even further.

Daniela Riley
mom to Will and Susana

Don't compare yourself to other moms! It gets intimidating thinking about your weight gain and comparing how other moms are doing things. Go at your own pace.

Sharon Auw
Jaedyn Auw-Colman's mother

For me, it is very hard not to compare babies since I have twins. I constantly see one baby do something and wonder when his brother will start doing it, too. For example, Eli started rolling over at 10 weeks old, and it took Seth awhile longer. So far, Seth has been about three weeks behind Eli in everything: tracking objects, smiling, cooing, etc.

I also find that I love to hear what my friends' babies are doing (or even strangers' babies for that matter), but I think it's just out of curiosity and interest more than anything else. I certainly don't think less of my babies if I find out another baby their age did something they're not doing yet.

LISA GREEN
MOTHER OF TWIN BOYS AND A GIRL

Questions:

Do you think it's wrong to compare your baby to someone else's baby? Why or why not?

In what area is your baby ahead developmentally? In what area is he or she behind?

CHAPTER 10-

Take Good Care of Yourself

A new baby adds a whole new level of demand on your time—and it can take its toll on your energy. Taking care of yourself is as crucial as learning to feed, bathe and soothe your baby. It is important for you to make sure you find time to get away and rejuvenate yourself. As my friends point out, it's not only nice to do so, it's downright necessary.

Sometimes I'll get a chance to sneak away and walk the dog with nothing but my iPod and my favorite tunes. Other times, I'll go all-out and really pamper myself at the day spa, which, for me personally, is the fastest way to rejuvenate myself. However, I don't often have the time or the budget for that. So I have had to find other ways to take a breather—or what I like to call a mini-vacation—during my day.

My first mini-vacation comes in the form of a nice, hot cup of freshly brewed coffee. Being a high-maintenance coffee drinker, I make sure I have plenty of my favorite French vanilla creamer on hand in order to start my day off right.

While I drink my coffee, I try to stay current with the world outside my home by catching the first few minutes of the TODAY show.

Since I work from home, if I don't have a scheduled phone meeting or pressing work to catch up on, my next mini-vacation comes during Kylan's first nap, which is my me time. And sometimes that particular vacation means taking a nap myself. After that, I'm off and running for the rest of the day, until Kylan goes to bed at night.

My husband and I try to connect with each other after our daughter goes to bed. However, it doesn't happen every night. And sometimes connecting with him just means sitting in the same room watching TV or surfing the Internet. Keep in mind that spending quality time with your partner is not only good for you but is also good for the baby.

I also love to light a few candles at night and sit either outside or in bed and read a magazine or a book while enjoying a nice glass of wine.

How others can help you, too

Within the first year of having my first child and moving to a new state where I knew no one, both of my sisters ended up moving near us. My husband and I have also been very fortunate to have had them live with us off-and-on during the last half of Kylan's first year. Kylan was the luckiest girl alive because her Mimi and Lulu loved her to death.

Taking care of myself also meant that I needed to take care and nurture the relationships around me, especially with my husband. Because we were still new to Nashville and didn't know many people, it was nice to have built-in friends (who happened to be my sisters) watch Kylan and take care of her so my husband and I could slip away and have some time for ourselves.

What other Moms have to say:

Allow your kiddo to have some time away from you. It won't kill 'em, I promise! You just might find that you enjoy him a little more after some time apart.

Angela Tuininga
mom of two: Benjamin and Leah

Make time for you and your husband. Babies can consume so much of your time and attention. Make sure you and your husband are spending enough time together to keep your relationship solid.

MANDY PHILLIPS
ELI AND JOSIE'S MOTHER

No one will ever care for your baby exactly like you will, but that's okay! I had a friend who didn't want to leave her baby in the nursery at church because the nursery worker held her daughter a different way. You have to be a little more flexible.

JENNA KUYKENDALL
RYAN, RACHEL AND SAMUEL'S MOTHER

Don't give up your old life completely. Becoming a mother means that, yes, in many ways your life will drastically change. However, don't cast aside all the things you once loved. Were you a passionate member of a book club? Stay involved. Were you an active runner? Take advantage of nursery services provided at most gyms or invest in a jogging stroller. Did you have a regular girls' night? Make sure it still happens! Participating in things like this isn't an indulgence—it's a necessity. Happy and healthy moms are the best moms. Your baby needs to develop the tools to be independent and you need—and deserve—a break!

MARY CADY BOLIN
MOTHER OF TWO GIRLS

165

In order to be a good parent—or even a great parent—and keep up with the demands of parenthood you have to take care of yourself. Remember to fill your own bucket before you run around filling everyone else's.

AMY BEAUDETTE
KEATON, ABBIE AND BRODY'S MOTHER

Providing time for yourself can be one of the most valuable stress relievers available for moms. Whether it's reading a book, going to the grocery store (alone), or creating a "girls' night out," it is important to be more than only "Mommy."

JULIE HONAN
EVAN AND AVERY'S MOTHER

First babies are very challenging for marriages–at least it was for ours. You're so exhausted after giving of yourself all day and all night to this little person who is utterly dependent on you that the last thing you want to do is give of yourself to your spouse. Yes, we survived and got through that first year, but not unscathed. It took its toll on us. Now I realize how important communication and time for you and your spouse really is. If you can (and it's so difficult sometimes) get away, go on date nights and spend time together, just the two of you.

Jaimie Schuster
Joseph and Madelyn's mother

I always tried to take a 20-minute rest a day, read a book, take a nap, take a shower or something that was just for me. I could have cleaned but knew how important it was to take some time for myself. My husband also made me leave the house once a week even just for an hour just to have a change in scenery. It helped a lot and still does.

Dana McCoy
Emma and Ethan's mother

Don't let children stop you from having a social life! They need to see you live a healthy, balanced lifestyle, which includes having mommy and daddy time or just mommy time with girlfriends. While your children are a huge part of your life, make sure you take time for yourself, too!

LINDSEY HOELTER
MOM OF TWO KIDS: THERON AND AINSLIE

QUESTIONS:

What kinds of things do you need to do for yourself so that you have more energy to give to your baby?

How can you make time to do those things?

CHAPTER 11-

Smother Your Baby with Love and Affection

I don't think any baby in the world got more kisses from her mom than my little girl. Her cheeks were just so kissable. I loved her great big smiles after each kiss which just wanted me to kiss those cheeks even more.

Even during the times that it was difficult to soothe her, I would try and give her many kisses to let her know that I was there and still loved her even if she was unhappy. Kissing her during those times also helped me to remain calm during a frustrating experience. And who knows, maybe she was crying because she wanted or needed affection or social interaction from me.

Comfort and Consistency

Some people may disagree that structure is an important aspect of loving and nurturing a baby. I was taught that if you have a regular feeding and sleeping schedule, your baby learns to trust you to feed her, play with her, and provide enough time for sleep. Therefore, I believe it is a good idea to set a routine for your baby as soon as possible. Being consistent in what you do is another way to show your love.

Babies develop trust when someone consistently cares for them. They come to know they can depend on the caregiver and thus a bond is created with that person.

Special Bonding Time

Feeding time is an ideal time to show love. I have heard that mothers who are closely bonded with their babies gaze at them more often and for longer periods of time than those who aren't. So when you are feeding or even changing your baby, make sure you and your baby only have eyes for each other. To make it fun, you can even turn it into a game of peek-a-boo.

Another way to show love and affection is by touching your baby frequently and holding him close as often as you can. The close contact soothes babies as it reminds them of the comfort of the womb.

A baby massage with lotion or oil is a wonderful activity. Massaging your baby enhances the emotional bond: it can calm, improve sleep, and also help in digestion. While you are massaging your baby, remember to be respectful and aware of what your baby is feeling. Stop if you sense over-stimulation. If your child starts to look away or squirm or gets fussy, it is a good sign that he has had enough. A newborn may enjoy only two to five minutes of massage, while a child over two months of age might enjoy longer.

Create little rituals that are special to you and your baby. For example, come up with a special song that you sing while bathing or rocking your baby to sleep.

WHAT OTHER MOMS HAVE TO SAY:

I've learned that firm words and a hug do more to teach and console than a firm hand and yelling.

AMY BEAUDETTE
KEATON, ABBIE AND BRODY'S MOTHER

As a speech-language Pathologist, and a mother of two talkers, it is extremely important to use as much language around your children as possible. While you are changing a diaper or putting on clothes, sing to your baby or tell them what you are doing. Although they may not understand every word you are saying, they are hearing the patterns of language.

Julie Honan
Evan and Avery's mother

My youngest, Avery, is one of the most strong-willed children I have ever come across. I think if she had been my first I would have been too scared to have had more! We are now finally seeing the positives of her competitive nature (learning to swim, diving off a high dive just to keep up with her sisters, learning to ride a bike without training wheels just so she could go faster than everyone else, and staying with a chore until it is done right). I really struggled with her at first, then when she was around the age of four God and I had a talk. It happened while I was at a conference for urban youth workers, where I met a beautiful, strong, Godly woman who led one of the workshops. As I was admiring her beautiful strength, God said, "Amy, you need to keep loving and training Avery in the way she should go. Her "strong" can look this beautiful for her someday, too." It just gave me a tangible picture of how God uses all personalities for His glory.

I distinctly remember feeling like the most important thing to do with her when I got home was give her a lot of affection. Avery wasn't a very affectionate child, but I knew there was a soft heart in there somewhere. I started by lying next to her and holding her at night for at least 10 minutes. After a few weeks of that, I saw a real change in her. There was a softness about her that wasn't there before, and also a need for affection developed in her. Now she is also great at showing others affection. My daughter, as it turns out, is a beautiful mix of soft heart and strength. I have learned to accept how God made her. I feel like instead of wanting her to be different, I have embraced who she is, and as her mother, I try to help her figure out how to get through life with such strong opinions about everything.

Amy Bowman
mom of three girls: Teagan, Colsie and Avery

The more positive attention you give your little ones the less likely they are to seek alternative methods (usually being naughty) to get you to pay attention to them. The more time I spend engaged with them emotionally, physically, and mentally, the more agreeable they are and the easier they are to be with.

Amy Beaudette
Keaton, Abbie and Brody's mother

Teach your kids in love! They don't know anything, and will have to start at the beginning. Answer questions. Kids are curious and want to learn, so explain as you go. Children are like sponges—they absorb everything. They also want to help with everything. If possible, let them. Maybe it will take you longer, but you will have one proud child on your hands when you're through!

Chrissi Helle
MOM OF TWO GIRLS AND ONE BOY

Our way of showing love and affection to our daughter is through words and actions. It's very important to tell your children you are proud of them, that they are doing a good job, but also to reinforce it through physical gestures like clapping, hugs and even some "high fives," which my daughter loves to get from her dad.

Melissa Jantzen
mom of Ada and Will

As moms, we are the center of our children's world. Starting the day off with a smile from Mom can make a huge difference in your child's day.

ELIZABETH HEDDEN
MOM OF THREE GIRLS: AVERY, KATHERINE AND WHITNEY

When your children ask questions, for goodness sake, answer them! My son, Joshua, has always been extremely inquisitive and curious. Furthermore, he has never been a child who is easily satisfied with the answer "because." If he has a question, he wants an acceptable, and preferably thoughtful, answer! As perceptive and brilliant parents, we discerned this trait in him at an early age and adopted the philosophy of always telling him the truth and explaining things the best we could. We had no idea how much was truly sinking in until the following exchange was relayed to me by his preschool teacher.

Apparently, the class of four-year-olds had been talking about things that God made. One little boy in the class courageously expressed his opinion, only to fall helplessly into Joshua's waiting snare. As the boy proudly professed that God had made pants, Joshua leapt into the conversation and corrected his classmate. Without hesitation, Joshua instructed the class that God had not made pants, but had actually made cotton. The cotton was then picked and turned into thread, which was in turn woven into fabric. That fabric was used to make pants, which we purchased at the Gap. After the lengthy explanation, Joshua passionately reiterated again that God did not, in fact, make pants!

Kristine Herring
Joshua, Nathan and Elizabeth's mother

I think babies especially need eye contact. They love face time with their mommy.

Daniela Riley
mom to Will and Susana

The best ways to show love and affection to your baby are the following: hugging, kissing, holding, smiling at them, talking to them, imitating their sounds, encouraging them with words in a soft tone of voice, tickling them, and massaging them with lotion after bath time.

LISA GREEN
MOTHER OF TWIN BOYS AND A GIRL

With my kids, I use hugs, kisses, laughs, explanations and books to show them that I love them. Each child is different, but no matter what happens—a scraped knee, a rainy day, a favorite toy in pieces—at our house, all can be rectified with one of the above. First and foremost, I am a lover, so my kids get tons of hugs and kisses—daily, hourly! If they are still upset, we try and make each other laugh. If that doesn't work, I pull out their favorite book and read it for the 905th time. When all is settled, we talk about it —how we can avoid it happening in the future, how we are going to "replace" whatever was damaged, etc.

Meredith Trullinger
mother of two girls

I have taken the time to learn my kids' "love languages." We as humans all have a dominant love language—the way we get our buckets filled, if you will. My son Keaton's love language is "acts of service." He shows his love by doing things for the people he loves. He loves to help. This allows me to engage him in, say, cleaning, cooking, or anything else around the house that helps out the family and allows him to show his love at the same time. He receives love this way as well. He loves it when you take time to "fix" his bike or help him plan a "party." My daughter Abbie is an affectionate little girl, and her love language is "touch." She loves to give kisses, hugs or even a smile to show others her love. She gets her bucket filled by cuddle time or tickle sessions. Knowing how to communicate your child's love language makes it easier to convey love to them.

Amy Beaudette,
Keaton, Abbie and Brody's mother

My husband and I don't like to start any conversation with "This is our *adopted* son…" as if we feel differently about our son just because he's adopted. If anything our 'adopted' son has more of a place in our hearts because we *chose* to pursue him. We fought for our son for months and on the day he came home with us for the first time, he became one of us. We hope to teach him that he can feel and act proud on the fact that he was adopted, that he was loved *twice* as much, that we 'picked' him to be a part of our family.

McKinna Murnane
adoptive mother to Leeland
and birth mother to Bridgman

QUESTIONS:

What are some of the ways that you show affection to your baby?

How do they respond?

What do you say to your child that confirms your love to him?

CHAPTER 12-

It's Off to Work I Go—Or Not!

Will you decide to be a full-time-stay-at-home mom, work part-time, or work full-time?

Since my husband was going back to graduate school just a month after Kylan was born, I had no choice but to go back to work while he was in school. I worked from home, so we took turns watching Kylan throughout the day. In the mornings while he was in class, I watched Kylan. Then in the afternoon, I went to work while he took care of Kylan. I had the best of both worlds. I could stay home with my new baby, and I could work. The bonus was I could often take short breaks to run out to give her a squeeze.

Since I knew I would be returning to work fairly soon after my daughter was born, I used my two-month maternity leave to work at getting Kylan into a routine that would fit, or somewhat fit, my regular morning business phone calls.

My situation of working from home was ideal. Plus, half the day, she was able to be with her daddy and I know that was a special time for both of them.

Making the Transition

The post-baby transition back to work can sometimes be very difficult. And for those of you who continue to breast-feed, it can be even more challenging. I have heard of moms who literally sit in closets at work to pump at least three times a day during their breaks. Now *that* is dedication and something I admire greatly.

Going back to work after maternity leave can create emotional conflicts for new moms. Working outside the home doesn't make you a bad mother. It's okay to look forward to the challenges and interactions of your job. Keep reminding yourself that you're doing what's best for you and your family.

If you are really struggling with being separated from your newborn, take comfort in the fact that going back to work does get easier for most women with time. Your baby will still know you are the mom and will love you just the same.

What other Moms have to say:

After my husband, Jason, and I had Emory, we wondered how we were going to afford day care. After some number crunching, we determined that it would be more cost effective to have one of us work part time and stay home with her the rest of the time. In our situation, I carried our family's health insurance and my husband was still in school. So, he found a part-time job working evenings on Thursday and Friday and every other weekend. So, after six short weeks after giving birth, I was back to work. Talk about tough! I was getting up three or four times a night breast-feeding, then working eight hours a day. I pumped three times a day at work. I was physically exhausted, and looking back, I have no idea how I did it!

Jason became the husband and father I knew he could be. It took a little coaxing to get him to put our daughter on a schedule (I had to write out when she slept, how much to feed her, and that she could not nap on him during naps!), but the two of them became two peas in a pod!

As much as I have always wanted to be a stay-at-home mom, God had a great plan in mind for our little family. Who knows what will happen when Jason finishes his master's in December and we try for our second child. Perhaps then I can be the stay-at-home mom I have always wanted to be.

Diana Likes
Emory and Finn's mother

My son, Keaton, was only six weeks old when I returned to work. It was the hardest thing in the world, and looking back on it, I missed out on so much with him. After Abbie was born, I stayed home for a year with her and Keaton. It was a challenge having a one-year-old and a newborn, but I was grateful for the many moments I had with both of them during that year.

Amy Beaudette
Keaton, Abbie and Brody's mother

When we first moved to Houston, I didn't think we would need my income, and was looking forward to being a stay-at-home mom. We soon discovered, however, that some sort of income on my part was necessary, and so I started working at our church part time. I was nervous at first that I would have a hard time balancing the work and kids, but now I am so grateful for the opportunity to get out of the house, put the kids in school/daycare, and have some adult conversations!

I discovered that I am not the type of person who can stay at home full-time without going insane. I need the social and intellectual stimulus that working brings. Being away from my kids periodically also makes me miss them and makes our reunions in the afternoons and evenings all the sweeter.

Jenna Kuykendall
Ryan, Rachel and Samuel's mother

Staying home after the birth of our first child was an easy decision for me because I had always wanted to be a stay-at-home mom. My husband and I felt like even if we had to give up doing certain things or wait on buying a home, having a parent at home for our kids was that important to us. Sometimes it is a struggle because we think, gosh, if we had two incomes we could do this and that. When it comes down to it, our kids are more important than having things. We figure that once they are in school, I can go back to work and try to be home when they get home. I have learned to treasure the time I have with them every day, going places, and doing things, and just being there for them. I see the difference staying home makes—at least in my own kids. So as long as we can do it, I will be at home with them.

Dana McCoy
Emma and Ethan's mother

I didn't want to go back to work when our daughter was born. The goals that my husband Tim and I agreed on, as far as how we wanted to raise our kids, made it virtually impossible for me to work at the same time. And that was totally fine with me, though I did eventually tire of it. I began to feel like I was disappearing because I didn't have meetings to attend or responsibilities outside of the laundry, dishes and the kids. So, I went back to work full-time when Bea was two and a half and Norah was one. It was a difficult transition, and there are definitely days now when I wish I hadn't! So you have to weigh your options and do what's best for you, even if that changes.

Jen Fischer
Beatrice and Norah's mother

I had what I now realize was a pretty cool job before I became a stay-at-home mom. I worked for a cable TV news channel, where I interviewed celebrities and political figures and sat in on some pretty famous courtroom trials. A college degree and seven years of experience brought me to where I was when I quit to stay home. But as far as parenting, I had two books and some high school babysitting experience to draw on. No one had prepared me for the transition from a noisy newsroom to the loneliness of sitting home with a baby who slept for 16 hours a day. I think if I had to tell people anything it would be to make friends with moms who have babies. Go to church, join a mom's group, do something, but make sure you get out with other people who understand that there will be days when you feel like your biggest accomplishment that day was taking a shower.

Go somewhere— take a hike, go to Starbucks, whatever. Even if it takes you an hour to get ready to leave and you're only gone for twenty minutes, it's worth it to have something to look forward to. One of the most fun things I did was to become a tourist in my own town. I looked up all the museums, arboretums, gardens, churches, and so forth, that I'd always wanted to visit but never had, and I took the baby. Make the most out of the time. It will be over all too quickly.

Laura Falin
mother of four

Thoughts and Other Advice

Use the next few pages to journal or make notes during this new stage in your life as a new mom.

And if you are giving this book as a gift, feel free to use this space to contribute your own advice, too! There's no better way to offer your support than to encourage a new mom who is just starting this journey.

We'd love to hear from you!

If you have some good advice you would give to a new mom and if you would like to be included in a possible future book, please go to **www.TheBestAdviceForNewMoms.com/Submit** and submit your information. If your advice is chosen, we will be in touch with you.

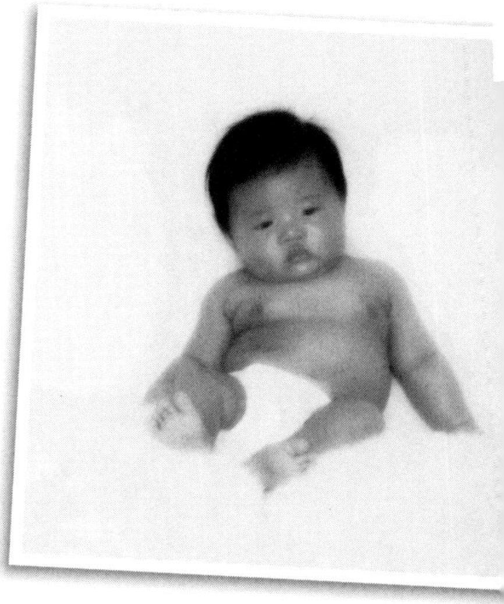

If you would like to order more books for baby shower gifts, new baby gifts or other for other new moms you know, please go to **www.TheBestAdviceForNewMoms.com/Book** and place your order. For bulk discounts, please email **jillc@edgehillpublishing.com**.